I
Hate
Weddings

A Minister's And Couple's Guide To Sacred Weddings

By John V. Carrier

Fairway Press
Lima, Ohio

I HATE WEDDINGS

392.5
C 31i
C . 2

FIRST EDITION
Copyright © 1993 by
John V. Carrier

7964 / ISBN 1-55673-541-3 PRINTED IN U.S.A.

How I dread preaching on the estate of marriage! I am reluctant to do it because I am afraid if I once get really involved in the subject, it will make a lot of work for me and for others.
                                                        Dr. Martin Luther, c. 1522

Acknowledgments

Thanks are, of course, due to many: to Wendy Wirth-Brock, who did a terrific job of proofreading my first manuscript; to Weyno Hager, Sherry Klitz, and Marlene Marks, who helped me write Gloria Dei's wedding guide booklet; to Gloria Dei Lutheran Church, of Neenah, Wisconsin, a congregation who has always encouraged its pastors to actively pursue continuing education opportunities, and thus gave me the time and money to work on this project; and to Trinity Lutheran Seminary, Columbus, Ohio, my Alma Mater, which provided me a place to stay, study, research, think, interact, and write. Thanks to Walter Bouman, Donald Luck, and Paul Harms, professors, mentors, and friends, who teach all who will listen that worship is vital ministry, and not to be trifled with.

This book is dedicated to Beth Heimlich, of whom my sister prophesied on the day before Beth and I were married, "Hang on to her John, she will teach you how to love." Nancy was right.

Soli Deo Gloria

I Hate Weddings

Foreword   7
Preface   9
Chapter 1
  Customary, But Stupid!   13

Chapter 2
  Making It a Sacred Occasion   29

Chapter 3
  Premarital Counseling: Insist On It!   53

Chapter 4
  Fee? Fee?   61
  Counseling Contract For Couples   68

Chapter 5
  Inexpensive, Not Cheap   71

Chapter 6
  Presents Or Presence?   81

Appendices
  A — *A Sample Parish Wedding Policy Booklet*   83
  B — *A Pastor's Wedding Planning Sheet*   90
  C — *Sermons You Can Use*   92

Recommended Readings   124

Bibliography   126

Endnotes   130

Foreword

There can be little doubt that there is often a discrepancy between what clergy learn in seminary training about their ministries, and what the larger culture expects of clergy. One very visible example of such discrepancy is the marriage rite. TV programs rarely show clergy, but when they do, it is often as benign functionaries at marriage ceremonies. The misunderstandings begin with the idea that clergy marry people to each other. Other misunderstandings build on this one. Church buildings are where marriages are supposed to take place. Brides wear white. They are "given away" by their fathers. The list goes on.

Hardly ever does anyone ask where these ideas originated or what they mean. Just as infrequently, couples planning their wedding rites do not ask whether these traditions reflect their own values and understandings; nor do they ask whether or how their Christian faith might be more appropriately reflected in their marriage rites.

This volume is designed to help Christian couples think about how their marriage rite might reflect Christian insight into marriage. The author knows the basics. The bride and the groom are the ministers of marriage. The state regulates marriage as a legal contract. Family and friends may gather to witness the public vows of the bride and groom. Up to this point nothing specifically Christian is taking place, and no clergyperson is needed. Judges and ship captains can function just as well.

Christian concerns are involved when we begin to speak about "blessing" a marriage. The Christian community is called to have a ministry to marriages, all marriages, and that ministry is life-long. The ritual is the signal that the Christian community has been about the business of preparing a couple for marriage. It is also a commitment by the Christian community to serve that marriage for as long as it lasts. The ritual itself is an act of "blessing" through the Word of God and

7

Christian prayer, through gestures and actions, through song and eucharistic meal. The Christian clergyperson is not "on call" to perform marriages at the request of all who seek her/his services. He/she presides over the Christian community's ministry to the marriage.

John Carrier has written this book to show how a bride and groom, a family and a congregation can think together about what they might do and what they need to do so that this ministry to marriage can take place effectively and appropriately. Entering into the spirit of this book will be disturbing and challenging. But to give oneself to consideration of the proposals will also be encouraging and rewarding. Onward and upward!

Walter R. Bouman, Professor
Trinity Lutheran Seminary
Columbus, Ohio
December 13, 1992

Preface

First, a confession. I do hate weddings. Marriage is great! But weddings! Weddings are the least favorite aspect of my job as a pastor. Many, maybe most, of my colleagues in ministry hate weddings, too, but they are afraid to say so in public, since most laypeople are simply "ga ga" about weddings. Even my clergy colleagues who love "doing weddings" will, when pressed, tell you they have to resist a lot of nonsense and fluffy sentimentality. Such a joyous time! But there is a lot to dislike.

One seminary professor friend, who likes weddings, says about the fluff, "Oh, well. They always want that. I just never give it to them!" Exactly.

How did we ever get ourselves into this mess, anyway? In the early Church, marriages were, more or less, established by the couple themselves. They decided to marry each other. It was not until the Council of Trent, in the mid-sixteenth century, that the Roman Catholic Church officially decreed that for a marriage to be valid, it must be performed by the clergy. For the rank and file, it was a civil agreement. The medieval priest was often called upon to bless the marriage bed, evidently to conjure the power of God to bless the couple with many children, and to ward off evil spirits.[1]

The priest was called into the occasion, all to often, to do his magic act. Sometimes the Church would bless or solemnize the civil arrangement. Indeed, up until the latter half of the twentieth century, most Protestant liturgies and hymnals refer to the occasion as "solemnizing."

The great reformer of the Church, Martin Luther, believed that marriages were a civil affair, "a worldly estate" and not a sacrament.[2] The Council of Trent decreed officially that marriage *was* a sacrament, due probably in no small part to this controversy of the Reformation. Luther did not prevail in this argument with Rome (nor in any other, for that matter), but in most Protestant churches, indeed, marriage is not a sacrament, but a rite. Today, in many countries, it is

9

strictly the state that presides over the legal contract, and the Church's blessing is sought only by the pious, and only after the marriage.

Now, in modern America, where the legality of common law marriages are recognized by the courts, I find myself wondering if the legal function of marrying in the Church is even necessary, much less desirable. Why should couples bother registering with the state? Sound far-fetched, and too radical? Consider the orthodox Quakers who continue to solemnize their own vows, no clergy needed, only witnesses.[3] Perhaps the Church should move toward presiding over the marriage of "members" only, and let those who seek to "live together" do so — with or without the blessings of the state. The state has so thoroughly turned over this function to the clergy, and the clergy have so thoroughly embraced the task, that it has lost almost all of its meaning, anyway.

Luther's observation that marriage is equally valid among non-Christians as it is among the baptized is obvious.[4] The Roman Catholic Church, and to some extent, certain other church bodies, maintain that marriage is a sacrament. And, it therefore follows that all of us who were not married in the Roman Church are not really married! This remains a bone of contention. The classic Protestant definition of a sacrament clearly excludes matrimony. A sacrament is instituted by Christ Himself, and involves both an earthly element, and the Gospel of Jesus Christ, thus being a means of grace. Matrimony fails the test in all categories. That we insist that Christians go about marriage in the unique way of Christ's love is only to be expected. This is how we are to live all aspects of life, making marriage no more a sacrament than, say the Christian entrepreneur! Yes, she/he must go about business with Christian principles, but that does not make his or her contracts sacraments! That clergy are to be about the office of Word and Sacrament calls into serious question as to just what the heck we're doing in our wedding practice.

The Church has need of great reform in this arena. Our ministry in the rite of matrimony is to help couples enter into a relationship founded in Christ. This is not the business of clergy alone, but all the faithful. We will never accomplish this if we offer a "hatch, patch and dispatch" service to all paying customers. Nor will we accomplish this if we continue to allow our culture to dictate our belief and practice.

Many traditions in modern American weddings are meaningless anachronisms, like coachwhip holders on horseless carriages. Most of our ritual practices are based on what the European nobility of a bygone era did, rather than on how 95 percent of the world's population lived. Much of ancient routine was based on superstition, and a world view that is, to say the least, pre-enlightenment. The world was flat, spermatozoa were little people which incubated in the woman, she contributing really nothing to her offspring, genetically speaking. Disease was the product of evil spirits. Women were the property of men, and in general had an oppressed and inferior position in all aspects of life.

Many standard trappings at modern day weddings are even pagan and occasionally barbaric in their origin. I hope this book will appeal to all you non-traditionalists who are searching for meaning and joy, and would like to sing a new song, and a better one than "Here comes the bride, all fat and wide. Here comes the groom, skinny as a broom."

Weddings are time-consuming work, and my time is precious. I work too hard as it is, and it irks me to have to put so much time into something taken so lightly. Give me a funeral over a wedding any day! Seriously! People attending a funeral are just aching to hear the Good News, to pray, to place themselves in the care of a loving God. People in a wedding want schmaltz and glitz, and they want to get it over with fast so they can party. Maybe you don't. If you are one of those rare individuals, then this book is for you. If, however, you are one whom I have just described in the above gross generalization, then please, read on; this book is *really* for you!

So, one whole chapter, and an overriding theme for this book will be: "making it a sacred occasion." This book assumes a Christian view without apology. Too often the choice of a church wedding is made because it seems like a nice romantic setting. This book is written, in part, for ministers who are tired of such abuse, and wish to recover (or discover for the first time) a more appropriate theology and practice in regard to weddings.

I have a friend who says, "I think it should be a whole lot harder to get married, and a whole lot easier to get a divorce." Maybe. In any event, it would be great if people would consider more carefully what it is they are getting themselves into before the wedding, and give themselves permission to get out while the gettin' is good. The pain of divorce is not to be underestimated, and if you can avoid it by not getting into a marriage that will not work, more power to you. Usually, that pain is intensified exponentially by the presence of children, who often suffer even more than the divorcing parents. Therefore, this book is not only about planning a wedding, but planning a marriage.

Weddings are frequently a terrific waste of the couple's (or their parents') money, too. Poor stewardship seems to be the rule when spending money on weddings. I, for one, am sick of it! It is a shame to see how much money folks spend on the few moments of their wedding, when it would be better spent on building a better marriage. So, another major aspect of this book will appeal to all who want to have a memorable wedding, but do not want to file bankruptcy.

Don't overlook the appendices. There are all sorts of goodies there, and as long as you don't try to claim them as your own, and make a ton of money off of them, feel free to copy whatever you like and use it to your heart's content. This includes the sermons. On all the sermons but one, I have removed the wedding couples's names, substituting the originals with names of people we (my wife Beth and I) love.

For Tina and Scoot, whom we also love, the names remain for sentimental reasons. On this wedding, dear daughter, we worked hard, and even fought long! I hope it was worth it to you. It certainly was for Beth and me!

Chapter One

Customary, But Stupid!

Several years ago, I was at a Roman Catholic wedding (not officiating). During the procession, the bride carried her bouquet of flowers to the shrine of Mary, the Mother of Jesus, and laid the flowers at the feet of the statue. I was close enough to the front to overhear the mother of the groom say, "Well, now that's different! I wonder what that's all about?"

One of her daughters leaned over and whispered, "She's offering up her virginity to the Blessed Virgin." The mother of the groom rolled her eyes, smirked, and said, "Oh, right!"

Flowers, and the throwing of fruit, nuts, rice, and now (out of consideration for church janitors and sparrows) birdseed, all hearken back to ancient, and mostly pagan, fertility rites. Some of these practices were also based in magical acts intended to ward off evil spirits.[1] While one of the basic functions of sex and marriage is bearing children, it is by no means the only one! God bless the infertile couple, and ease their pain of longing and undue shame! Too long have we held fertility as a measure of worth, often especially the woman's worth, assuming that the infertility is due to her inadequacies and not the man's! And God bless the couple who chooses not to have children because they know that they would not make good parents, or who voluntarily choose to halt a genetic disease. We have plenty of people in this world, and far too many unwanted children. Let's take care of those we have!

Like it or not, this is the origin of the bride carrying flowers at the wedding: she is symbolically carrying her "flowers" to give, not to St. Mary, but to her man. Not only was the above mother's cynicism justified, but there is a basic fallacy here. Marriage is more than just giving sex to one another! Marriage is more than matching genitalia; it is combining people. "Two become one." It is establishing a community within

13

the larger community. For Christians, it is establishing a community of Christ within the larger community of Christ: the Church. There is a whole collection of traditions surrounding virginity that range from the silly to the barbaric, and many of them, we are still doing today. Why? Not because we value virginity, but because it's cute.

Until recently, the white wedding dress was the sole prerogative of the virgin. Now, thankfully, any color of dress goes for any woman. But wedding garb still has many of the trappings of some ancient nonsense. Ever notice how wedding dresses are somewhat similar in design to lingerie? That's mostly because this is precisely what it used to be. The woman was presented to the man in her underwear, his sexual prize, in many instances, bought or stolen. The whole history is rife with male dominance and double standards.

The wearing of modified white underwear is not only a symbol of "purity," and the sexual act that will end that purity which is assumed to be the unique property of female virgins. It also has the history of being the "proof" of the maiden's virtue, which in some cultures is/was paraded publicly! The blood-stained sheets from the bed, on the night in which she was wed, were at the very least examined by the mothers of the bride and groom, mostly as proof that the man got what he paid for: a virgin. In some cultures, these proofs were hung from the bedroom window, or paraded through town on a pike.[2]

The shame, and the resultant public humiliation, punishments, and social disfavor that would result in an insufficient show of blood that was produced on a maiden's wedding night, led to many bizarre and sometimes dangerous methods of guaranteed bleeding.[3] The fact that bleeding due to a torn hymen is a "largely unreliable" sign of virginity, made urgent these methods of "faking" it. That there is no analogous means to prove that the man is/was virginal, made it all the more inconsequential, as nobody really cared!

Let's digress a little on this subject of virginity. There are two reasons for virginity before marriage: fear and grace.

Mostly, we are inclined toward the fear. Today with sexually transmitted diseases (STDs) on the rampage, and the plague of HIV which leads to AIDS, there is a lot to be afraid for, even your life. This is nothing new. Smallpox was so-called in Europe, because as deadly as it might have been, it was nothing compared to the "Great Pox" of the time: syphilis![4] The only sure way to avoid getting these diseases, when they are sexually transmitted, is to not have sex with anyone! When you do have sexual intercourse, pick one lifetime partner who is also a virgin.

There are other aspects of the fear motivation. No one wants to get pregnant before they are ready to have children. There are some pretty reliable methods of birth control, and there are some terribly unreliable ones, too. Just as there are some fairly reliable prophylactics against STDs. But almost nobody uses these methods the first time they have sexual intercourse. So, again, the way to avoid getting pregnant before you want to, is to not have sexual intercourse.

In a recent study of 17,024 couples, it was " ... found that cohabitating couples had significantly lower premarital satisfaction compared to couples where the two people still lived alone before marriage .... Almost two-thirds (64 percent) of the cohabitating couples fell into the low satisfaction group, whereas almost two-thirds (64 percent) of the couples where both partners lived alone fell into the very satisfied group .... This study also found that couples that live alone before marriage seem to have the best premarital relationship, which we have found is also predictive of later marital success."[5] In the sixties and seventies, the prevailing wisdom was, "Find out if you are compatible before you get married!" It made a lot of sense; we'd seen the misery so common in marriage, and we wanted to make sure we were right for each other before taking the plunge. But it evidently was a social experiment that does not work for most people.

Some years ago, a pastoral counselor friend declared the following: "You don't really start working on being married until you are married. Couples that live together before they are married are mostly just using each other." Ouch! Strident. Generalizing. Overstated. Possibly true. I am reminded of how some people purchase cars. Unless there is a commitment to lifelong fidelity, test-driving your marital relationship might actually be a self-deception based not on an intention to "buy into" marriage, but to get a few miles in as a free rental.

As I write this, I am aware that this is a rather crass confrontation. I am aware of the pain I feel internally, as I take on a new set of thoughts that I did not (could not? would not?) hold before. If you are feeling something akin to this, rejoice! For you have been called into the struggle.

Another fear motivator is maturity. When I first had sexual intercourse, I was not ready! I thought I was ready, but I was wrong. Premature sex (which differs from premarital sex) is a sure cure for happiness. Teenagers and preteens simply are not ready for sex. Premature sex arrests the maturing process. It took me many years to realize this, and many more to recover from it. I have seen, known, and cared deeply for a great many teenagers. Many of them have been terribly hurt by premature sexual activity. I do not know which came first, the chicken or the egg, but I do know that there is a link between premature sex, cigarette smoking, and alcohol and other drug abuse among teens, which of course also relates to violence, and suicide.[6] (For more information on risk behaviors and teens, see several excellent studies from Search Institute, 122 W. Franklin Avenue, Minneapolis, MN 55404 (612) 870-9511.)

God has made promises of great rewards to those who are chaste. We are challenged to find out what these rewards are. Some of these rewards are found in the double-negative of the fear motivations: no unnecessary, inordinate fear! No STDs, no unwanted pregnancies, no arrested maturing process because of premature sexual activity. But beyond this there is more. There is the possibility of living a chaste life, under the way that the Scriptures indicate is God's intention for us. Living according to God's will, and not in rebellion against it, is its own reward.

Thankfully, we have a God who does not base our relationship on our behavior, but on the grace established through His Son, Jesus of Nazareth, the Christ! Because you are not a virgin at the time of your wedding does not mean that God has abandoned you, or loves you any less. Far from it. God is constantly chasing after us sinners, no matter what form our rebellion or brokenness, or victimization has taken. If this is not true, then we are all going to hell in a handbasket.

It is not hopeless! A joke: Do you know the difference between a human being and a lightbulb? You can unscrew a lightbulb!

You cannot unscrew even yourself! But God can! It is never too late to receive the grace of God and start over. Some counselors are talking now about "rediscovered, or reclaimed virginity!" Of course you will never forget your first sexual encounters, not really (unless they were so traumatic that you have repressed the memory), but you can deal with the past, and start over.

Virginity before marriage is good. This does not mean that a couple should be naive (see the chapter on premarital counseling). Sexual naivete can be a terrible problem for a couple, but there is a lot of joy, excitement, and fun in getting to know your partner sexually. If sexual activity is difficult, painful, or frightening for you and/or your mate, please do not hesitate to get qualified help. If nothing else, find a good book on the subject.

In an important work, *A Community of Character*, Stanley Hauerwas[7] explores our modern family structures and the ensuing ethics. This book is not the place for repeating work that he has already done. Suffice it to say it is a piece worthy of our attention. With mostly gut feelings as our only resource, we assume much that "ain't necessarily so."

"The issue becomes not really whether the family will continue to exist, but what kind of family should exist, and what moral presuppositions are necessary to form and sustain it (p. 156)."

Hauerwas (p. 159) points out that while we assume that the so-called nuclear family has its foundations in stated commitment, its actual base is more one of biology. The family is our form of continuing the species. We are linked at the hips by forces of nature, more than we are consciously moved to love. [Here I mean love in any sense: emotional (*philos*) or conscious decision based in the Gospel (*agape*), though some call *libidos* "love."] As screaming Tina Turner demands, "What's love got to do with it?"

Again, Hauerwas: "Unless marriage has a purpose beyond being together, it will certainly be a hell. For it to be saved from being a hell we must have the conviction that the family represents a vocation necessary for a people who have a mission and yet have learned to be patient. Marriage and family require time to love one person rather than many ... (p. 172)."

Hauerwas is here not opting for one model of family structure, nor even insisting that married people have children. Rather, he is right to say that if we are in "significant relationship" as Christians, be it as spouses or as parents, we have a moral obligation to use that relationship to consciously improve the world. This is a particularly urgent task when the relationship involves having and rearing children. More from Hauerwas:

"Current reflections about sexual ethics by Christian ethicists is a mess. By rights, theologians and ethicists should not be able to say enough good about sex. Broad anthropological analysis has shown us that we are fundamentally sexual beings and that is indeed a good thing. God has created us to be sexual beings and it seems nothing short of Manichaeanism for us to deny that aspect of our lives (p. 175)."

We are pointed to a very important arena in which we must slug out this sexual ethic: the Christian community. Is our self-ethic constructive or destructive of the Church and society as a whole? Surely it cannot be considered neutral or having no effect. Merely the amazing amounts of time and money which we spend on the subject clearly indicate that not only do we think sex is important, but that we (all of us) are profoundly affected by sex, whether we want to be or not. No matter how private sexual activity may be, it is never strictly a private thing. The welfare of the community is always involved, because we are communal animals. We are connected to each other. Christians have a special calling to this truth as the community of Christ within the larger world community.

Sexual infidelity, for example, has remarkable powers of destruction. Entire extended families can be ripped apart because one member of that family engaged in a sexual activity outside his/her primary relationship. Teen pregnancies can and often do, "ruin" not only mothers' and infants' lives, but affect many others as well. (Yes, I know there are notable exceptions, and congratulations, but these are the exceptions that prove the rule.) I have already mentioned the devastation of sexually transmitted diseases. The point is: it is not just individuals who are hurt, but the entire community.

Conversely, our sexuality is important for positive reasons, as well. Sexual fidelity, committed and exclusive relationships, delayed sexual intercourse to the time of solid (and public?) commitment between mature persons, and children raised by parents who take steps toward becoming "good" at child-rearing, are sexual ethics whose practice elevates us all. Attaching guilt to this already burdened subject of "family" is not very helpful. (Guilt is only helpful if it can motivate to appropriate action, and in the process of acting relieve the guilt.) But conversely, attaching a sense of communal contribution, dignity, and joy to a sexual ethic could only be good.

We have the romantic notion that having sex with someone is a necessary expression of commitment and love. Many people confuse intimacy with sexual expression, and seem to have difficulty sorting out the two. Sexual intimacy is also often viewed to be necessarily at a certain stage in the progression of the relationship:

1. Meet.
2. Hold hands.
3. Kiss.

4. Kiss with tongues (not the same as glossolalia!).
5. Petting.
6. Heavy petting.
7. Sexual intercourse

But with just a little thought, it is obvious that there are many committed, intimate, and truly wonderful personal relationships that never even get to "first base." Many stages in this progression are not only *not* necessary ingredients to intimacy, but in fact, in most of our relationships would be quite detrimental, if not downright destructive. For example, what place is there for these progressive stages in relationships with children, your pastor, your closest colleague, your sibling(s), parents, parishioners, racquetball partner, etc.? Why then do we assume that progressing inexorably toward sexual intercourse will necessarily help our relationship with a boyfriend or girlfriend? Even if they have "progressed" (yet another assumption!) to being fiancees, is sexual intercourse before marriage necessarily good for the relationship, much less for the relationship with our Christian and global communities?

Countryman[8] very rightly makes the connection between virginity, chastity, and a man's property rights in Biblical times. Adultery and property are closely linked in ancient patriarchies. If one's property goes to one's legitimate heirs, then he'd better be darned sure that the children (especially boys) are indeed his. Women, therefore, are included in the list of property which we men are prohibited from coveting. Nowadays, we do not say "wife" but more inclusively, "You shall not covet your neighbor's spouse." This broadening of the original intent of the 9th Commandment is very appropriate for our time, but it is a deviation from at least part of the original purpose: to preserve the patriarchal society by outlawing adultery. Specifically, adultery was narrowly defined as a man having sex with someone else's wife (or betrothed). It was not considered adultery for a man to have sex with a female slave, prostitute, concubine, or divorced or widowed woman. Why? Because it did not violate anyone's propery interests. For similar reasons, it was considered adultery to have sex with a virgin to whom you were not betrothed or married, because this violated her father's property interests (pp. 158-9).

The point of all this is not to throw out the baby with the bathwater. The Bible is still the living Word for us today. But as Countryman points out, we cannot apply 2,000-year-old-plus concepts to all modern circumstances, and expect them to function well, much less the way they functioned then. As much as we want to have a Bible-based sexual ethic, it is not entirely possible, or even desirable.

The fundamentalist view that every word of the Bible is a word for all time is simply untenable. This is true for possibly all things, but the parameters of this book (marriage) are particularly constraining. Still, despite our resistance, Christ and His Gospel break into our time and culture just as surely as they did in first century Palestine. Perhaps our most urgent task, as Christians who are interested in marriage and a sexual ethic, is not so much to engage in a once-and-for-all quest, from which upon its completion we may rest, but rather to always be engaged in a tireless and never ending conversation with the Word. Engage in the struggle!

The Christian community is challenged: "Will they make their existing purity codes conditions of salvation, or will they acknowledge that they have no right to limit what God gives? (Countryman, p. 243)." We Christians may find sexual purity useful for our own lives, and may even find these codes to contribute to community, but as those who live in the grace of the Gospel, we have no right to make these codes a (much less *the*) condition for admission to the Church and salvation.

Having said all this, LISTEN! Virginity is not a precondition for marital satisfaction or happiness. Virginity is not something that is good for the woman, but inconsequential for the man. Virginity is not a fair criterion for the judgment of someone's character, or worth as a prospective spouse. Virginity is not magic, as the ancients believed, and many people still maintain today.

If you are concerned because you are in a relationship where one of you is/was a virgin at the time of your marriage, and the other was not, fear not! Your partner's virginity, or the lack thereof, will not make him/her any more or less fit as a mate. You do not need to worry about one person's previous experiences, or inexperience. The relationship you must be concerned about now is yours! Unless there is some unfinished business in a previous relationship, do not worry about it; get on with your life.

God help us if we are not beyond the time of the sacrifice of virgins to volcano gods, building bridges on the bones of a virgin,[9] or the requisite of a virgin to carry my weapons of war thus giving them efficacy against my enemies! And God help us, because we are not past the era of double standards for the genders, and because we men still have a desire to sexually conquer the vulnerable young virgin! The sin of patriarchy continues!

The patriarchal form of marriage was founded in the custom of "purchasing" a bride, which itself may have been a practice evolving from paying recompense for having stolen her from her family in the first place.[10] In any event, this practice of purchasing a bride is found in many primitive cultures to this day, but has holdovers in more modern and Christian cultures, as well.[11] Indeed, the very origin of the word "wedding" derives from a security of money or property, called the wed. "Thus originated the term wedding, or pledging the troth of the bride to the man who secured her by purchase."[12]

This continues to be played out when the father of the bride "gives the bride away." Until recently, this was a part of many, if not most, religious ceremonies:[13]

"Then shall the Minister say, Who giveth this Woman to be married to this Man?"

> *"Then shall they give their troth to each other in this manner. The Minister, receiving the Woman at her father's or friend's hands, shall cause the Man with his right hand to take the Woman by her right hand, and to say after him as followeth ...."*
> *The Book of Common Prayer*[14]

Once and for all, let's disabuse ourselves of the notion that women are property! No one *gives* anyone! If a woman wants to be escorted to the altar by her father, why not by her mother as well? While we are at it, why not both sets of parents escorting their children to each other? This has a much more positive and loving message to it. Mothers and fathers have done their job to this point. They now drop back from parenting their children, and take on the new responsibility of being supportive family members of an adult, married, couple. Part of that new job will be something very important, and very difficult: the task of doing *nothing* . . . the task of keeping hands off when it would be so easy to interfere.

Of course, more and more, we are seeing yet another option. No one escorts anyone. The bride and the groom meet either in the rear of the chancel, and process in together (as do all the couples in the wedding party), or the men and women process in separately, and meet in front of the chancel, near the altar. In either case, the message is clear: the couple is joining of their own accord. They enter into this covenant of their own free will, and on their own volition.

Personally, I am heartened by the moves we make away from sexism and patriarchy. I think I can back my joy with some pretty steady theology and biblical scholarship. Sure, women's ascension to equality (and the necessary descent of men to a proper sense of humility) has seen its share of problems, but what hasn't? No movement of human beings has been without sin. But the women's movement has not been especially sinful, and the overall outcome is something very good. The least that can be said is that some bad things about the way the sexes relate are slowly being put to rest.

Weddings, and more importantly, the ensuing structure of the marriage relationship, need reform in the area of sexism. The greatest perpetrators of sexist wedding customs are the women who themselves insist on such things. We men, and we Christians both male and female, need not feel threatened by equality and liberation. Just because everyone else is doing it does not mean *we* must. From early on, we have confused our cultural norms, and age-old customs with higher Christian ideals.[15]

The wearing of wedding rings is an old symbol and very traditional in Judeo-Christian cultures. Egypt, 2800 B.C., is the oldest record we have of the wearing of wedding rings.[16] Although gold is today the traditional material of choice, many other metals, and even non-metals have been used. The ring, being a circle, has been taken to symbolize eternity and fidelity. The ring, especially when only the woman wears one, has also been taken to mean a loss of freedom, ownership, and being on the left hand (the less powerful), a symbol of servitude.[17] According to one school of archeology, rings are thought to date to the time of enslavement of women, and were the actual instrument of their bondage. More and more, we are moving away from this attitude, and toward shared responsibility and faithfulness. A mutual bond, not of slavery, but binding commitment, is therefore expressed in a double ring ceremony. A single ring expresses something less. Don't ask me what no rings represent.

It used to be that a ring was required. This is no longer the case. If occupation (some jobs make the wearing of rings very dangerous) or personal taste, or finances, make the wearing of rings undesirable, don't feel bad about it! You are just as married, with or without rings.

Going overboard with your wedding jewelry is no more appropriate than overspending in any department. Simplicity is the key. Opulence will only impoverish you, and distract everyone from recognizing Christ in your life. The importance of a ring is considerably less than the importance of your relationship. If you want rings, fine, but there is no Christian significance to them. The blessing of rings, as is so common in the Roman Catholic tradition, has no scriptural or theological foundation.

Most people recognize that the ever popular bridal veil has roots in a time when, at least royal weddings, and in some cultures, all weddings, were arranged at childhood. The bride and groom were hidden from each other until the actual wedding. The groom saw what he (or more likely his father) bought only once she was unveiled at the altar. We kept this tradition long after arranged marriages went out of style. We did so by remembering an associated superstition. How often have you heard it said that it is unlucky for the groom to see the bride on the day of their wedding until she is marched down the aisle? The veil may also have had an important magical role in warding off evil spirits, as was the white cloth the bride walked on believed to prevent the evil spirits from rising up from the earth and invading yon fair maiden! I wonder if it may not also have had to do with keeping feet and clothing clean in a less-than-sterile medieval church setting! Painting, and otherwise disfiguring the wedding couple's vehicle, and hanging from it tin cans making noise, may be a lot of fun, but these practices likewise doubtless have their origin in warding off the evil spirits.[18]

Panati[19] tells a more sordid history, again portraying the general oppression of women. The wearing of veils, not only during a wedding, but before and after, and by all women, was the cultural norm for much of Europe and Asia. Certain Islamic cultures maintain this custom today. Women, married and unmarried, were to be hidden from view of all males, other than their husbands. That this resulted in social and economic oppression was just fine with the men who made the rules in the first place!

Bridesmaids date back to the age of brides being mostly stolen. Even if the bride knew her "captor," and wanted to be caught, it was unseemly to give in too willingly. So it was that she was protected by an entourage of helpful sisters and housemaidens who tried to save her honor. Yes, the "maid of honor!" Nowadays, the holdover is many women processing up the aisle before the bride, delaying her approach as best they can. We have come from a real-life struggle, to some fun pretending, to a pompous and meaningless ceremony.

Ah, but let's not forget the groom! In today's American wedding culture, the bride is the focus, and the groom is almost perfunctory, a mere necessity. It is a truly seductive power trip to be the bride — queen for a day!

Sometimes I almost think that if a woman could get away with having a wedding without a groom to go with it, we might have a few takers. But it is not to be. You must have a groom to have a wedding. He comes with his "best man," and as Panati[20] points out, only the best man is up to the task! You didn't think he could storm the bride's father's house alone, did you? And once making off with his stolen prize, what's to prevent her kinfolk from coming and just taking her back? Five strong men: his groomsmen.

Want to know why they are all similarly, if not identically, dressed as the groom? To protect them from evil spirits by confusing the demons as to which one is the right one to befuddle on his wedding day![21]

I suspect that even the bachelor party, which not long ago was traditionally held the night before the wedding, and now is replaced most often by the rehearsal dinner, may have a throwback to this same period of marriage by theft and purchase. The man gets together with his drinking buddies, and after liberal lubrication, they find the nerve to do the dirty deed. A raucous time, I'm sure, perhaps even fun on occasion, not infrequently dangerous and frightening, and today lacking much value.

I always regret hearing reports of bachelor parties. Perhaps as I age I need to remember my more youthful, and considerably wilder days. But I've grown intolerant of Christian young men getting drunk and going to strip joints, and even on occasion hiring a whore for the groom. I know it might be fun, but it is not innocent fun. I think it is important to gather with friends and celebrate, and maybe even grieve, the changes that are sure to come in this new life together. But are we Christians, or not?

You know, after just a little research, we start to recognize that many of our traditions in weddings really have no worth at all, except that they are traditions. Learning this can become a little disheartening. But it can also be liberating. If there is no good reason for doing something, then you are free to not do it! It's optional! Now you are free to do what truly is meaningful and important to you, without all the extraneous distractions and expenses. This is particularly important to the Christian.

I do not believe that there ever was a time when it was easy to be a faithful follower of Christ. When we are joined to Christ in baptism, we join in the struggle! There have been many times and places where it has been easy to be complacent about one's faith and discipleship. These times have often proven to be more challenging to faith than the times of harshest persecution. Late 20th century America is a time of great difficulty for the faithful. For us, it is " . . . the cares of the world, and the lure of wealth . . . . " (Matthew 13:22) that prove to be our thorniest problems.

If we are to stand any chance of being faithful followers of Christ, repentance (*metanoia*) will be a necessary component of our life. I am not talking about salvation by doing God's will. I am talking about a faithful response to all that God has done for us. A faithful response necessarily includes joining in the struggle for what is good, and against what is evil. Things that are empty of worth or meaning, including cherished cultural customs, are evil. The harm they do is in appearing to be harmless distractions, when actually they distract us from that which has real worth and meaning, in particular, Jesus Christ.

To the bride and groom:

A few words about the reception. In some respects, this is the time for frivolity and nonsense. Anything within reason, decency and dignity could be allowed. This is the time for sentimental songs that have no direct bearing on God, or the love of Christ. Popular romantic songs, from just about any source, are certainly acceptable here. Silly fun, like throwing your bouquet, and/or garter belt, cutting and eating wedding cakes, and all that sort of thing belong here, even if their origins are a bit tainted.

Similarly, carrying the bride over the threshold, not part of a wedding, but the honeymoon, seems an innocent enough custom, and is now taken as an honoring of the bride by her new husband. But the origin of this ancient practice is far from innocent! Actually documented by Plutarch of Rome some 2,000 years ago, it is in memory of the rape of the Sabine virgins by Romulus (after whom Rome is named) and his army! The women were literally carried off by force and taken as wives. It is a fascinating story,[22] but hardly one Christians would want to memorialize, much less repeat!

Having said all that, stop and think! Everyone is watching you! What is it you want you and your guests to most remember? Luther asked a very important question over and over again in his Small Catechism, and it applies to everything we say and do: "What does this mean?"

Chapter Two

Making It A Sacred Occasion

In a recent clergy journal, one veteran pastor proclaimed that no matter how hard the minister tries, it is impossible to make a wedding into a sacred occasion. If this is true, then I want no part of it as a minister of the Church. Just do your own thing, and send me an invitation. I'll send you the obligatory gift, and we'll get it over with as quickly and as painlessly as possible. If we are close friends or kindred, I will attend the ceremony and grit my teeth, but please do not ask me to preside! My job and my identity as a pastor require me to witness to the Gospel and the Kingdom of God, even when I am having a good time with family and friends. To ask me to do less than this borders on abuse.

Please, please, please! Just plan something as sentimental and as superficial as you want, ask the justice of the peace to wear whatever costume you desire, and do it! It really is okay! But don't ask me to dress it all up in some sort of religious wrapping paper! The Church has much too important a job to do (the mission of Jesus Christ) than to be wasting its time and resources by confusing itself and everyone else with all of our cultural wedding baggage.

What can couples and clergy do to break away and violate the 11th Commandment: "Thou shalt not make weddings a sacred occasion?" I think it can be done, detail by detail. Basically, all we really need to do is pay attention to what we are doing, and what we are saying. Let's start with the service, the ceremony itself.

The pastor's ministry is actually the ministry of the Church. The Church has entrusted the ceremonial ministry of weddings, and some of the pastoral care, to specially educated and designated persons we call clergy. But if the ministry of the Church stops here, we do marriage and the Church a grave disservice. Congregations should spend some time studying these issues of marriage preparation, Christian ritual, appropriateness of customs, etc. But the ministry to marriage does not stop there. In Christian rites of marriage, we pledge ourselves in prayer, blessing and (with Holy Communion) sacrament. We therefore must ask how we can help the relationship that we ritually reinforce.

Friend Walter Bouman, of Trinity Lutheran Seminary, Columbus, Ohio, says that we in the Church are to be "Marriage Cheerleaders." Can we come to understand ourselves (I mean all believers, not just clergy) as being in a lifelong ministry to all marriages? If not, then one of my basic contentions is underscored: if couples are coming to the Church merely to rent the hall and the services of a religious, freelance justice of the peace, then they should be sent elsewhere. But if the couple is interested in joining the Church in the Christian marriage enterprise, then they are to be welcomed as partners in ministry.

In pre-marriage counseling (which by the way, I require if I am to participate in the service), I routinely ask the couple to write their own vows. We may not use what they write; we will almost certainly re-write and edit their compositions together, but it is a very helpful exercise. I ask the couple to write what they wish to communicate at their wedding: "Write down what it is you want to say to him/her, and what you want the congregation and the Lord to hear about your plans for your marriage." I ask them to do this independently, without consulting one another.

This is sometimes very easy, and sometimes difficult. Occasionally, I will need to meet with each person privately to help them express their ideas in writing. Usually, the difficulty is one of literacy. The bride or groom is not skilled in written communications, so we talk, and I try to summarize what the person is trying to say. At this stage in the process, I am straining to contain myself, and not commenting on the content, but just trying to help the persons express their thoughts in writing.

We get together, and they read aloud to each other what they have written. This is often a very touching and spiritual occasion. "I never knew you felt that way!" is often the result. At this moment, I am fulfilled! One of my goals is to get the couple to say what has been in their hearts, but not on their lips.

Often, this exchange is just a rehash of something they have seen or heard in a traditional service, and that's okay. At the very least, the couple has stopped to consider what is going on and what is being said, rather than mutely standing by while they "get married." That is just too passive. Something is being done to them, and they have little input as to what it is! Instead, they are active participants; this is something they are doing to and for each other. They will be saying, "I married Beth (or John)," rather than, "We got married on June 19th."

Indeed, the *Lutheran Book of Worship*[1] recognizes this, and affirms that marrying another is the action of the couple by this proclamation: "Dan and Audrey, by their promises before God and in the presence of this congregation, have bound themselves to one another as husband and wife."

The next step in this process is to help the couple see the need for adding to, or correcting their vision of what their marriage vows mean. There are some minimum standards to which the Church ascribes, and therefore, in order to be a Church wedding, must be met. The first, and most obvious is a pledge to fidelity. Somewhere in their vows, the couple must promise that they will be faithful to each other.

> *Ah, love, let us be true*
> *To one another! For the world, which seems*
> *To lie before us like a land of dreams,*
> *So various, so beautiful, so new,*
> *Hath really neither joy, nor love, nor light,*
> *Nor certitude, nor peace, nor help for pain.*
> — *Matthew Arnold*[2]

Faithfulness, of course, has many facets. When God established Israel, the covenant was described as a marriage. The People of God had basically this one duty in the covenant:

31

to be faithful. This meant no other gods. And when people were not true to this covenant, they were described as faithless adulterers. The prophet Hosea lived out this accusation by taking a whore for a bride. (See also Ezekiel, especially chapter 23.)

In any partnership, basic to being faithful to that person is having no other alliance that damages that primary relationship. I state this premise in this manner, because there is more to faithlessness than just having sex with someone who is not your mate. Sexual adultery is, of course, a way of being faithless. Surely sexual adultery violates the trust, or faith, basic to the relationship, but it is only one way of being faithless among many ways on a long list.

If faithlessness is having a relationship that violates the primary relationship, then it is adulterous to have a relationship with alcohol or other drugs, if that comes between you and your spouse. It is an adulterous relationship with your means of employment, if you spend so much time and energy at work that you end up with not enough time and energy (or none at all) with your spouse. (I've listened to more than one pastor's wife lament that the Church is her husband's "other woman.") You can have adulterous relations with just about anyone or anything, even good things! Just as you can have sex with someone who is really a good person, and still be committing adultery.

Even more slippery, but maybe just as important, is the adulterous relationship you can have with yourself. If you are the center of your universe, so much so that your needs to be angry, or sad, or entertained, or busy, or churchly, or alone, or ... whatever gets between you and your spouse, then this is how you commit adultery. I have personally committed adultery this way, and I have seen many others commit adultery with: work, school, church, food, children, PTA, volunteer fire department, service clubs, riding clubs, and golf clubs, the kids' activities, even writing or reading good books like this one!

Whew! That was a long way of getting around to my point: the vows of marriage must say something about faithfulness. And, they should say something about what happens when we violate this trust.

What does happen when something interferes with your marriage? Is that it? Finito? Not for Christians! We recognize that marriage is a wonderful gift from God, but that we are good at messing up just about any gift the Lord has to offer. Somewhere in our vows, there ought to be a recognition of sin, and a remembrance of grace. That is basic to all that is Christian: the Gospel!

The *Lutheran Book of Worship* has a wonderful introduction to the vows:

"The Lord God in his goodness created us male and female, and by the gift of marriage founded human community in a joy that begins now and is brought to perfection in the life to come.

Because of sin, our age-old rebellion, the gladness of marriage can be overcast, and the gift of the family can become a burden. But because God, who established marriage, continues to bless it with his abundant and ever-present support, we can be sustained in our weariness, and have our joy restored.

(name) and (name) if it is your intention to share with each other your joys and sorrows, and all that the years will bring, with your promises bind yourselves to each other as husband and wife."

If this type of statement is not present in the ceremony, I maintain that it cannot be truly a Christian wedding. All the trappings and trimmings can be present, but if an expression of the Gospel is missing, then it may well be a religious ceremony, but it is not Christian. So, in writing our vows together, we come to the "what if."

I ask the couple to consider in writing their vows, "What if it doesn't work out in the way of your dreams?" What if you do not feel the love you promise to have for her forever?

What if you fail to be faithful, and are drawn to another man? What if your spouse falls ill, and you just can't handle it? What if he seems to be offering you a lot more than you are offering him? What if you cannot provide the things you promised? What then? As the couple shapes and reshapes their vows, they move toward mutuality, realistic promises and goals, and an articulated promise of grace.

Here is an example of what one couple came up with:

> **Beth, I vow to you, with God, our families and friends as witnesses, to love you as I am able all my days. In every circumstance, I vow to you to be true. I will, as I am able, provide to our needs as a family in matters of faith, love, security, health, and worldly fortune. I ask of you two things: to vow to me the same, and to forgive me when I have not honored these vows which I today pledge.**

> **Further, Beth, it is my deepest hope to make you truly happy in our life together, for it is this which makes me happy. I wish to be the father of your children, son to your parents, brother to your brothers and sisters, and husband and friend to you.**

> **I give you this ring as a sign of my love and faithfulness.**

> **I shout with Joy to God in heaven for blessing my life with one such as you!**

And then, of course, Beth promised the same to me. Shelby and Jason had this to say:

> **I take you Shelby/Jason, to be my wife/husband to have and to hold from this day forward. In the presence of God, our families, and our friends as witnesses, I promise to honor and respect, to love and be faithful, to support and forgive, to cherish and hold for as long as we both shall live.**

Tina and Scoot vowed:

I take you, (name), to be my wife/husband, and these things I promise you: I will be faithful to you and honor you; I will respect, trust, help, and care for you; I will share my life with you; I will forgive you as we have been forgiven; and I will try with you better to understand ourselves, the world, and God; through the best and worst of what is to come, as long as we shall live.

(I think they copied that one from a book.)

One ingenious way a pastor friend of mine uses in setting the tone of worship at weddings is to have one of the ushers lead the procession with the processional cross. This visually makes the statement, loud and clear, "The guest of honor is not the bride, not the groom, not the pastor, but Jesus Christ."

There are, of course, other ingenious innovations to get this message across. In liturgical churches, there is usually a Christ candle present. Lighting a marriage candle (sometimes called a unity candle) from the already-lit Christ candle symbolically returns the focus to our Savior. A soloist or duet singing "I Will Sing the Story of Your Love, O Lord," or some similar song, further drives home the point: it is not the radiance of the wedding couple, but the light of Christ which illuminates this marriage, and gives us hope and joy. Accompanying words such as the following could be said by the couple, or the presiding, or assisting minister: "Jesus Christ is the Light of the world; the light no darkness can overcome. Lord, Jesus Christ, let Your light shine through us that the world may rejoice in Your love."

A very wise and wonderful friend of mine recently noted of the Church; "We've brought grace to divorce, and it's about time, but we've brought almost nothing to marriage! How dare we take away romance? No, romance alone will not carry the day, but we almost celebrate its passing! 'Hasn't happened to you yet? Well, just wait, it will' "

How can we help love endure? Grace.

Having just now promoted extensively the concept of writing one's own vows, let me extend a caveat. Homemade vows can be as clumsy and rickety as homemade furniture. They demand some skillful crafting if they are to go beyond shallow and sentimental silliness.

Traditional vows have a certain value that many homegrown varieties do not. When we invest in tradition, we invest in the past. We join the human race. We enter into the common struggle in which marriage has endured and thrived for a very long time. Doing something novel for novelty's sake is no more valuable than doing something traditional for tradition's sake. If I could sum up the point of this book in one phrase, it would be this: be careful and considerate of all you do.

Scriptures

Perhaps those of us who do not include in our Bibles the various books that make up the Apocrypha should expand our vision to include at least this:

There are three things
in which our souls delight,
And which are delightful to God
and to all people:
Concord between brothers,
Friendship between neighbors,
And a wife and husband
who are inseparable.
— *Ecclesiasticus 25:1-2*

The reading of the Word is indispensable in any worship service. A worshipful wedding is no exception. Care should be taken to select scriptures that are appropriate to the occasion and the couple. Some scriptures seem perfect for the occasion, though they are not, taken in context, about marriage. For example, Ruth's words to Naomi (Ruth 1:16-17):

> *Do not press me to leave you*
> *or to turn back from following you!*
> *Where you go, I will go;*
> *Where you lodge, I will lodge;*
> *Your people will be my people,*
> *and your God my God.*
> *Where you die, I will die —*
> *there will I be buried.*
> *May the Lord do thus and so to me;*
> *and more as well,*
> *if even death parts me from you! (NRSV)*

Surely, these verses express the faithfulness we are looking for in a Christian marriage, but the text is Ruth's pledge to her aged mother-in-law, Naomi! The question is, do we preach the Word out of context, or not?

Take, for another example, John 2:1-10: though its setting is indeed a wedding, the passage has nothing to do with marriage! The minister and the couple, especially the preacher, need to decide if they wish to run the risk of reading unintended double meanings into the scriptures, in order to meet the worshipful need of Biblical readings. The dearth of readings for weddings, especially Gospel texts, presents us with a problem. Do we read only texts whose original context and intent apply to weddings and marriages, or may we choose readings that sound appropriate only when taken out of context? Perhaps the latter is permissible, if we do not do violence to the intent of the original, and as long as sound Christian doctrine is likewise upheld.

Doubtless, the most popular reading for weddings is from First Corinthians 12:31-13:13. Yet this writing has nothing to do with weddings! We stretch the capacity of this text to apply it to marriage, but I am not sure this is a mistake. The chapter is about Love, to be sure, but is addressed to a community divided against itself in a controversy over charismata (extraordinary gifts of the Holy Spirit). Paul's exhortation was to not think so much of your gifts (such as healing, or speaking in tongues) when you lack the gift of love, in particular, the uniquely Christian quality of *Agape*. In expounding on 1 Corinthians, the preacher should take care that what s/he preaches is on *agape* in marriage, and not romance, or other types of love that we experience.

Similar pitfalls are found in John 15:9-14. Jesus gives us His new commandment, to love one another, even as He has loved us. So it should be the love of Christ we preach, even at a wedding, and maybe especially at a wedding!

Having said all this, I present the following list of scriptures which people have often found to their liking at weddings. It is by no means an exhaustive list of possibilities. As part of pre-marriage "counseling," I ask the couple to read all of the listed scriptures, one text per day, as a daily (or nightly) devotion: "Talk about each text. What does it say or not say about your relationship, and your future marriage?" They are instructed to choose the lessons that are most appropriate to them and their life together. Often, we look for a Psalm, another Old Testament reading, a New Testament reading (non-Gospel), and a Gospel lesson, but not necessarily. They need not have all four and may choose only one. If the expected congregation is one accustomed to liturgical worship, we may sing the Psalm.

Suggested Readings

Psalms: 33, 100, 117, 127, 128, 136, 150
Old Testament:
  Genesis 1:26-31
  Genesis 2:18-24 (include vs. 25?)
  Ruth 1:16-17
  Song of Solomon (Song of Songs) 2:10-17 (omit vs. 15?)
  Song of Solomon 8:7
  Isaiah 60:19-22
  Isaiah 63:7-9

New Testament:
Romans 12:1-3, 9-13
1 Corinthians 12:31-13:13 (or a portion thereof)
Galatians 5:22-26
Ephesians 5:21-33
Philippians 1:27-2:5
Philippians 4:4-7 (8-9)
Colossians 2:6-7
Colossians 3:12-17
Hebrews 13:1-6
1 Peter 1:13-16, 22-25
1 Peter 3:8-9
2 Peter 1:3-11
2 Peter 3:11-15a
1 John 2:12-17
1 John 3:18-24
1 John 4:7-12

Gospel Lessons:
Matthew 19:3-6
Matthew 22:34-40
Mark 10:2-9
John 2:1-10
John 15:9-12
John 17:11, 15-19

Wedding Prayers
based on
Ephesians 3:14-19, and John 15:9-12

[Plain type is read by Presiding or Assisting Minister; **Bold type is the response of the congregation.**]

Let us pray for Michael and Arlene in their life together, and for all families throughout the world. Please respond to each petition: **"Fill us with Your love, O Lord."**

O God, source of Love, all good gifts come from You. Bless Arlene and Michael with the fullest measure of Your grace, that they may ever rejoice in the gifts You give them through each other. We pray to you,

"Fill us with Your love, O Lord."

Thank you God, for the gift of marriage. Thank you for giving us the innate desire to bond with another. Sometimes those bonds become strained under the burden of sin, sickness, riches, poverty, and busyness. Bless Michael and Arlene with courage, wisdom, strength, patience, affection and understanding, that when times are difficult, they may be for us, and for the world, a vision of Your reign that is to come. We pray to You,

"Fill us with Your love, O Lord."

Michael and Arlene have asked us to be part of their marriage by taking part in their wedding. Strengthen us in our relationships that together, we may support them in all ways, and they may be so filled with Your presence, that we might likewise be blessed by them. We pray to You,

"Fill us with Your love, O Lord."

Lord Jesus Christ, You have promised that Your joy will be in us, and our joy will be complete, if we will but trust Your word, and obey Your command to love each other. By the power of Your Holy Spirit, grant us the strength to love one another, as You have loved us. We pray to You,

"Fill us with Your love, O Lord."

Not all people are married, and not all will marry. This, too, is part of Your design for creation. Bless all single people with an equal sense of Your love. Help us to recognize single people in our midst, and to offer them all the love, support, and friendship that we offer our married friends, such as Arlene and Michael. We pray to You,

"Fill us with Your love, O Lord."

We pray to You, that being rooted and established in love, we may have the power, together with all the saints, to grasp how wide, and long, and high, and deep is the love of Christ. We pray to You,

"Fill us with Your love, O Lord."

We pray all this in the name of the Father, and of the Son and of the Holy Spirit.

Amen

Just as the above prayers include a petition for single persons, it is especially appropriate to pray for those who have suffered through the pains of divorce. Yes, it is tragic that today so many marriages end this way. Not having the perspective of God, I cannot truthfully assess if this is better or worse than when couples stayed married but miserable. In any event, the Church is called to convey the Gospel to all people, especially the hurt, the broken, and the oppressed. Public ministry to and for divorced persons must be included in this Gospel task. To shun or condemn the divorced is totally out of keeping with the love expressed by our Lord Jesus. For the divorced, and the children and parents of the divorced, weddings can be a particularly lonely and painful time. The Church's sensitivity to all the children of God on this occasion is a uniquely powerful opportunity that we should not pass up. It is in this spirit that I offer this prayer, composed by friend, colleague, and professor, Rev. Dr. Donald Luck:

Loving God, You forget nothing that is good. You reject none who turn to You. Look with compassion on those whose lives have experienced the disintegration and pain of divorce.

Bring to fulfillment in You everything in those former relationships of marital and family life which has been pleasing to You. Cover all with Your forgiveness and renewal. Let the warmth of Your grace melt away all bitterness and guilt. And to all who have experienced harm, grant wholeness of life, and new paths to walk under Your guidance and care; through Jesus Christ our Lord.

Amen

Prayers should be inclusively and sensitively worded. Prayer should offend only evil. Here, I risk sharing with you a prayer I recently encountered at a Roman Catholic wedding. Please do not use it!

" ... **we humbly pray to You for this bride who today is united with her husband in the bond of marriage. May Your fullest blessing come upon her and her husband ...** "

Why not pray for both of them to begin with? Everybody is now focused not on Christ, not on marriage, not even on the bride and groom, just the bride. Why should the Church endorse the wedding industry's mythology?

Here is a responsive form of the Lord's Prayer, the newlywed wife and husband leading the congregation.

Wife and Husband: Our Father in heaven, hallowed be Your name.

Congregation: All creation reveals Your glory. May all creation sing Your praise. We give thanks that through Your Son, Jesus Christ, we too may call You "Father."

Wife and Husband: Your kingdom come; Your will be done, on earth as in heaven.

Congregation: Grant us a full measure of Your Holy Spirit that our wills may be Your will. Make us tools of the Spirit for building peace, justice, and love. Through us may the world have a foretaste of everlasting life with You.

Wife and Husband: Give us today our daily bread.

Congregation: You know our every need, and still You have commanded us to come, that in our asking, we confess our trust in You. We confess that You know our needs, and trust You will meet our needs, all according to Your gracious will.

Wife and Husband: Forgive us our sins as we forgive those who sin against us.

Congregation: Move us to forgive those who do us wrong. Move us to forgive as completely as the forgiveness we receive through Your Son, Jesus Christ.

Wife and Husband: Save us from the time of trial.

Congregation: Never let us stray from You and Your kingdom. Though we may hear siren songs of temptation, tune our ears to Your voice. Give us strength, courage, and wisdom to follow you.

Wife and Husband: And deliver us from evil.

Congregation: When confronted with evil, from without or within, help us not lose heart, nor place our trust in false gods, false hopes, and empty promises, but always trust in You.

Wife and Husband: The kingdom, the power, and the glory are Yours, almighty Father,

Congregation: Now and forever.

All: Amen.

That's Music! Music! Music!

I guess that the "Bridal Chorus" from Wagner's "Lohengrin" (you know: Dah, dum dee dah. Dah dum dee dah . . .) is okay. It is just musical notes, after all. But what do you think, or sing to yourself when you hear this tune? I can't help think, "Here comes the bride, all fat and wide. Here come the groom, skinny as a broom!" I don't know, maybe it's just me. And then when I hear the "Wedding March" from Mendelssohn's "A Midsummer Nights's Dream," other silly images invade my psyche, like that game show, "The Newlyweds."

If you suffer from similar subliminal invasions, maybe you would do better to choose equally magnificent music that conveys a more magnificent message. There are marvelous pieces for organ or other instruments by such renowned composers as Bach, Brahms, Cesar Franck, Ralph Vaughan Williams, and Handel, to name but a few. And there are some marvelous hymns, as well. Some are great as processionals (**P**), others as recessionals (**R**), and still others as solos (**S**), or a thematic hymn (**H**) sung at a particular spot during the liturgy. Here are a few I recommend regularly. (The numbers listed refer to the *Lutheran Book of Worship*.)

    #16 I will Sing the Story of Your Love (**S**)
    #221 Sent Forth By God's Blessing (**R**)
    #245 All People That On Earth do Dwell (**H,P**)
    #253 Lord Jesus Christ Be Present Now (**S**)
    #287 O Perfect Love (**S,H,P**)
    #315 Love Divine, All Loves Excelling (**P,H,R**)
    #451 The Lord's My Shepherd (**S,H**)
    #456 The King of Love My Shepherd Is (**P,H,R**)
    #459 O Holy Spirit, Enter In (**S**)
    #474 Children of the Heavenly Father (**P,H,R**)
    #481 Savior, Like a Shepherd Lead Us (**P**)
    #518 Beautiful Savior (**P,H**)
    #534 Now Thank We All Our God (**H,R**)
    #543 Praise to the Lord, the Almighty (**P,H,R**)

#548 Oh, Worship the King **(P,H)**
#549 Praise, My Soul, The King of Heaven **(P,R)**
#557 Let All Things Now Living **(P,R)**

I am sure there are plenty of others not included in this list that will serve well. A particularly appropriate hymn not found in the *LBW* that I particularly like is John Ylvisaker's "I Was There To Hear Your Borning Cry."[3] Another hymn that is exceptionally suited to a wedding is from the Episcopal Church's hymnal: "Come Away to the Skies," (#213, Middlebury.)[4]

Organists may wish to examine their repertoire for "sacred music" fit for the occasion. Here are two resources which may be helpful, that run along the traditional lines:

Five Hymn Improvisations for Wedding and General Use. arranged by Paul Manz. St. Louis, MO. Morning Star Publishers. 1989. Publisher's no.: MSM-10-850

Frysell, Regina Homen. *Wedding Music.* American Guild of Organists. Rock Island, IL. Augustana Press. 1956.

There are simply scads of volumes and sheets of music, some of which are new, and suit modern tastes and instrumentation. As in all times, our era is no different: much of what is created is junk, but there are also many gems hidden in the trash. Go digging for the gems. Don't be satisfied with trite and shallow words or music!

To reiterate my point, what we say and do in this ceremony will convey a message. Everything we say and do and sing and play, should, therefore be meaningful, and mean what we want to express. If something is meaningless, it should be omitted.

As Elizabeth Swadley pointed out some years ago,

> *"A wedding today is not necessarily Christian because the ceremony is performed in a beautiful sanctuary or because the vows are solemnized by a minister of God or because the music is all 'church music.' These are all elements of a Christian wedding, but they do not make*

45

the wedding Christian. To make a wedding Christian, Jesus Christ Himself, through the Holy Spirit, must attend and be in evidence."[5]

The Eucharist:
Holy Communion
With A Wedding

What other way is Christ more truly present than in the Sacrament of the Altar? What better expresses unity than Holy Communion? How can we give greater thanks and praise to God than through the Eucharist? Why not surround the occasion of your wedding with the real presence of Christ?

Holy Communion not only does all this, but can provide a ministry like nothing else can. The family that is estranged can be led to forgiveness and reconciliation. The couple's unity in Christ is cemented sacramentally. The unification of two families is now made evident in Christ. Denominational differences can be conquered through our oneness in the Body and Blood of Christ. And the foundation of a community in Christ (the new marriage) is seen within the larger community of Christ, the Church. The entire body of Christ, and not just those assembled for the wedding, are in communion committed to the well-being of this marriage relationship, and therefore, at this meal, pledge their support.

A few words of caution. Care should be taken not to make non-communing members of the congregation feel unduly excluded. If there will be many present who are not Christian, perhaps the Sacrament should not be offered. Sensitivity to denominational differences is also appropriate. One should not violate one's own denominational guidelines without careful consideration. The minister should determine whether or not to celebrate the Eucharist through careful discussion with the couple. If yes, it is helpful to discuss the significance of the Sacrament during the sermon, and somewhere in the service, give clear directions as to how the congregation will proceed from their pews, what method of distribution you intend to use, and by what route to return to their places. Much of the hesitance to receive Holy Communion in a strange setting comes not from a religious reluctance, but from the fear of looking stupid in front of all these people!

The celebration of the Eucharist necessarily directs the focus of the worship toward Christ. The involvement of the entire congregation in an activity of worship, therefore, is required. It is very appropriate to include the newly-married couple in some assisting ministry, including the offering and distribution of the bread and wine. Nevertheless, the focus must always remain on Christ, and not the bride and groom.

Frequently, this is how I distribute Holy Communion at a wedding. The bride and groom come forward to the altar. Holding the bread, I say to them both, "The Body of Christ, given for you." I then hand the bread to one of them, and they give each other the bread, tearing off a piece (or a wafer — which I almost never use) and saying to each other, "The Body of Christ given for you." Sometimes, the couple will "feed" the bread directly to their mate, thus displacing that silly business with the wedding cake, and claiming a sacred feeding. Likewise, the cup of wine: "The Blood of Christ, shed for you."

Then the congregation. If there is a center aisle, the congregation proceeds up the center aisle to the presider, who gives them the bread (always with the words, "The Body of Christ, given for you.") They then move to their right or left to receive the wine from the bride or the groom, who are standing not together, but to either side. If the congregation is seated with the bride's family and friends sitting on one side, and the groom's on the other, I have them serve on the side opposite to their own. This way, the bride serves her in-laws, the groom his wife's best friends, etc. It can be a powerful experience! A new unity in Christ is symbolically expressed. The couple should rehearse this, of course, and be able to clearly say to each communicant, "The Blood of Christ, shed for you."

Note: It is imperative that the entire congregation of Christians be invited to receive the Body and Blood of Christ. Never is the couple alone to receive the Sacrament! This is the meal of the community of Christ, and not a private affair for the bride and groom. See appendices for wedding sermons with Holy Communion.

One of the most important functions of the clergy is to speak the word of God. When faced with the crisis that disrupts so many relationships (marriage), it is simply good pastoral care to invoke the power of God's will. The will of God is that marriages would first of all "work," that is, function well. A blessing from God's representative says, among other things: hands off! What these two people are doing is a good thing. "What God has joined together let no one put asunder."

We also speak God's promises. "The Lord bless you and keep you . . . . " God, by the power of the Holy Spirit, speaks this promise through the pastor. The giving of a blessing is not so much the minister's blessing (though it may be that, too), but God's blessing. It is a promise that God, through God's people, will help this relationship remain holy and intact. It is a promise made for God and for God's people, voiced by the minister.

Now, just exactly what is going on in a church wedding? Is this sacrament? Is this legal contract? License for sex? A familial rite of passage? What?

Augustine: "The word comes to the element; and so there is a sacrament, that is, a sort of visible word." (Augustine, *Commentary on John*, 80,3.) According to Robert Jenson,[6] as early in Church history as Tertullian, sacrament was the standard terminology for " . . . any publicly binding religious act (p. 291)." This rather loose definition could therefore apply not only to the two sacraments (Baptism and the Eucharist) as, for instance, Lutherans ascribe, and to the seven rites of the Roman tradition which that denomination calls sacraments, but also to the blessing of furnishings for use in worship, the commissioning of teachers and congregational officers, the reception and dismissal of members, and so on, *ad infinitum*, as long as it was public, religious, and binding. Well, be that as it may, what the Church *decides* is sacrament is an important consideration.

What informs this decision must be in part that which is unique to the Church. Clearly, Baptism and the Eucharist (Holy Communion) are unique, in that they are specifically expressions of the Gospel. Marriage, on the other hand, is anything but unique to the Church. That we find marriage important in our personal and corporate lives, and that through marriage we can participate in the world community in a special way as married Christians, does not elevate marriage to a sacramental level. Marriage is a vocation — a calling. The same is true for any vocation; be you an auto mechanic, teacher, or merchant, what you do as a Christian should be unique in the world, but the act of initially becoming a Christian mechanic, teacher, or married person, does not qualify as a specific and unique word-made-flesh sacrament, a visible word, one of the means of grace.

Sacraments are legitimate only if perfomed by the Church. Baptism, the Eucharist, and confession and forgiveness in the name of Jesus Christ, are both unique to the Church, and legitimate only within the Body of Christ which is the Church. If one outside the Church were to enact what looks like a sacrament, this would not make it so, no more than would a sacrament be administered if it were part of a dramatic stage presentation. Correlative to this, I think, is a rite of marriage. Marriage outside the Church is valid, and must be respected as such. A wedding outside the Church is not sacrament, and yet is legitimate. Similarly, a marriage between a Christian and a non-Christian is still a valid marriage, and not a sacrament. Can there rightly be a time when a sacrament is not a sacrament? Is, therefore, a wedding a sacrament just because it is an event in the Christian community and between two Christians?

This discussion could take us far afield from where we need to go. Dogmatists and ethicists will continue the struggle, I'm sure, long after you and I are dust. The subject of marriage and sacraments must be brought to the ecumenical debate, for it is no small matter, and of considerable pastoral concern. Too often, divorced persons seeking to remarry have been turned away from the altar, not because the couple's intent is suspect or spurious, but because the Church's or the minister's sacramentology is either too broad or too limited.

Because once done, a sacrament cannot be undone, Roman Catholic clergy have too often been required to demand from their members some rather dubious, and often painful, procedures in order to satisfy canon law. Persons come away from these proceedings with the impression that the Church is saying that their first marriage was not merely a human failure (sinful?), but invalid and illegitimate from the start. The agony of this rather imposing view and practice is compounded when there are children involved. I have heard many people come away wondering, "If my first marriage was invalid, does that mean that our children are bastards?"

So, the question, is marriage a sacrament, is still an important and current one. Schillebeeckx[7] (pg. 332) gives a complete (and I found it somewhat humorous) historical accounting of medieval theologians who struggled mightily with this issue. At its heart were two problems: 1) does marriage convey the grace of God, and 2) if marriage is a sacrament, can it be dissolved, undone, reversed?

The answers to the first question are a real kick! Marriage, in most circles, was recognized on two conditions: mutual consent, and sexual intercourse. A church that has great difficulty with sex at all found it problematic, to say the least, to suggest that the grace of God was conveyed in such a manner. Attempts were made to state that marriage was a sacrament only when it was Christians "doing it," but that had its usual problem of recognizing the validity of all marriages, even among those not baptized. Someone even suggested that it was a sort of sacrament, and it conveyed a little bit of grace! Definitions of sacrament have always assumed that it is God acting, not humans, but here was a sacrament that could be celebrated by two people by mutual consent and sexual consummation! It was a theological nightmare. No one believed that marriage was salvific, but if it was a means of grace, it had to be.

The second problem was only a little less thorny. Ever since people started forming bonds, they have been breaking them. When the Church started dealing with marriage, it immediately had to somehow deal with divorce. If marriage was a sacrament, how could one undo the means of grace? One could forbid the parties from remarrying, and thus do something akin to excommunicating them, but what sense does it make to exclude sinners from the means of grace? For whom are the sacraments intended, if not sinners?

But by the Middle Ages, matrimony was on the official list of seven sacraments, and once on, it had to somehow be justified. To the reformers of the Church, from Luther on, this simply was an error. We in the Church, especially as denominations, are not good at admitting errors and falling into the merciful arms of Christ. Sin happens in marriages and in the Church. Why can't we rely on the true means of grace, Christ's death and resurrection, and be done with it? Start over!

Please note, now, that this entire issue was, and is, dealing with the Western Church: Rome and the reforming churches that followed and splintered from Rome. In the Eastern traditions something else entirely was going on. Not encumbered by a legalistic view of marriage as a contract, nor by an essentially negative view of sex, the Eastern Churches were on a different track.

In the East, Christians married primarily as a familial rite. As in the West, the Church blessed the union whenever the bishop or priest came round to congratulate the couple (conceivably, months later). This very quickly developed into formal liturgies of betrothal, the bridal procession to the groom's house (as in Jesus' day in Judea; see Matthew 25:1-11), and the handing over of the bride to the groom. Certain customs, though pagan in origin, were adopted into the Christian rites. The state recognized the legality of Church marriages much earlier than in the West.

But back to the Western Church with which we are primarily concerned. It all came to a head at the Council of Trent, where it was officially decreed that a priest must be present as a witness for a marriage to be valid and binding. The idea was to intervene against clandestine and forced marriages. Consensus, that is, mutual consent, was a must. Unfortunately, as with any legalism, there were loopholes. If the priest was present even if by chance or by force, the wedding was valid. It was not until 1907 that the priest was required to actually hear the consensus himself: "I do."[8]

The Roman Church, after the Reformation, was in something of a quandary. Were Protestant and mixed Protestant-Roman Catholic marriages valid? Were they sacrament? Many decrees were passed down, each trying to solve a problem, and each often creating more. The final legal clause that gives me the greatest difficulty came in 1907, when Pope Pius X decreed that all Roman Catholics, even those married to non-Catholics, were to be married under the Roman Catholic legal form if their marriages were to be considered valid. This is especially unfortunate, given the fact that the intent of these rules was not to inhibit ecumenism, nor to put undo suffering upon "mixed" marriages, but to prohibit clandestine weddings, especially those in which one or both of those being married did not fully consent.

Another problematic, and rather modern, decree by Roman Catholic authority drives the wedge even further. Pope Pius IX ruled that marriage was essentially religious at least in part, and therefore, purely secular (courthouse, etc.) marriages between baptized Christians were indeed invalid (Canon numbers 1016 and 1960).

So, Christians, let's talk.

Chapter Three

Premarital Counseling: Insist On It!

Alas! is even love too weak
To unlock the heart, and let it speak?
Are even lovers powerless to reveal
To one another what indeed they feel?
— Arnold[1]

If you are a clergyperson, insist that the couple undergo some sort of premarital counseling before you will preside over the service. If you are unskilled, or unwilling, or do not have the time to do this yourself, arrange for someone else who is qualified to do it for you. Group experiences have been helpful for some, others have turned to ordained colleagues, and still others have entered into cooperative ventures with a local or regional social service agency. Whatever the method, some good, sane help, advice, and education about relationships is never a poor investment.

If you are one who is planning to get married, again, insist that before you say ''I do,'' you and your beloved will give this gift to your marriage! If your clergy does not do pre-marriage work, or is not qualified, and you must pay for this service, consider it money well spent. It is a much better investment in your marriage than almost anything that you will spend money on for your wedding. The wedding is only a few minutes; your marriage is forever.

I did not want one word of advice about Everett, myself, or the married state. I awaited marriage as revelation. I no more wanted a pre-marriage resume of what lay ahead than I want an inventory of Christmas presents before Christmas. I intended to launch into the state of Holy Matrimony unnourished by so much as a crumb of worldly knowledge; and I did so launch. The trouble was,

Everett was launched in exactly the same manner. And what we were headed for was not so much a collision course as a complete miss.

Jessamyn West, A Matter of Time[2]

I'd like to recommend a fine book for persons preparing for marriage, and for those whose job it is to help prepare them. It is by David Robert Mace: *Getting Ready for Marriage*. Nashville, TN. Abingdon Press. 1972. His insights are keen, and his writing is clear and easy to read. The annotated bibliography alone is worth the price of the book. Here is a quote from his preface:

> *We allow people to drift into this relationship, with all its maddening complexity, on pink clouds of romantic sentiment. We send them forth, after solemn ceremonies involving the blessing of religion and the hearty goodwill of relatives and friends, on a joint enterprise concerning which we have made no serious endeavor to enlighten them; and in which, as the dreary statistics make plain, a substantial number of them are doomed to fail.*

An old friend of mine says that he thinks it ought to be a whole lot harder to get married, and a whole lot easier to get divorced. There is some wisdom here, even if it is a bit overstated. This is the most serious commitment we can enter into. It may lead us into parenthood, and the responsibility of life itself for those too small to make decisions on their own. It may lead to joint ownership of many items of property, joint legal obligations, relationships with in-laws that we may or may not like, and to locations unknown. Yet for $50 and an "I do," you can jump right in, headfirst! Driving a car, selling real estate, and giving people backrubs at the "Y" require training, certification and licensing. But not marriage! And yet, when we get married, and it must end, we must go through tremendous pain and expense, and often legally required counseling, before we can get a divorce. Why? Because we take marriage seriously? Give me a break! If we really took it seriously, we would more adequately prepare ourselves for this most significant relationship of our lives. But often we do not prepare at all.

I think there are many reasons for this reluctance toward premarital counseling. The primary motivator is embarrassment. We are terribly private people! We think that matters of the heart and body are best kept in a dark closet, and only looked at, or experienced at all, when the shades are drawn. God forbid that we would look at ourselves in the light of day, and in the presence of another, "stranger!" This is further exacerbated by an embarrassing suspicion that we are inept at relationships, and poor performers sexually. For some reason, we believe that these are things that just come to us "naturally," and if we are found deficient in any area, there is something wrong with us.

This is not a helpful approach. Love is mostly a learned behavior. Unless you and your spouse both came from absolutely perfect homes, you are unlikely to have every tool needed for the job in your personal kit. If you are naive in any aspect of your relationship, why not get help with some education? You would never think of learning to drive a car by trial and error, would you? No, we think nothing of intentionally learning from others what it takes to operate a motor vehicle. In fact, the law insists on it! So why is it so difficult to bring ourselves to learn to relate to one another? Collisions in marriages are no safer than those on the highway, and sometimes, to my way of thinking, they can be much worse! So take a course in marriage relations, and be safer and happier than you are behind the wheel!

Mace[3] rightly asserts that good marriage preparation should take three forms:

1. Basic education. What do we need to know that we haven't learned about life together? Or, what have we learned that will not help, but hurt our marriage?

2. Evaluation. What is it about myself, my partner, and our relationship of which I/we need to be aware?

3. Counseling. Getting help with specific relationship issues that may become problematic.

One of the basic goals I have in pre-marriage work is to help the couple break through what some have called "Idealistic

Distortion." Bowman[4] points out that this is the big difference between dating and being married. In dating (an important part of preparing for marriage, at least in our culture), the couple works very hard at impressing, pleasing, and winning over their mate. Couples frequently spend a lot of energy "hiding" from each other. There is usually no intentional dishonesty or malice involved; it is just the way we court. I suspect that there are also some deep-down feelings of inadequacy at play. Our poor self-image says, "You could not possibly love the real me."

So it is that we often enter into marriage somewhat deceived, and somewhat deceptively. Our expectations of each other, and how life will be together, are unrealistic, and out of balance. So, when reality hits, it is a great disappointment. Exploring unrealistic expectations, and being prepared for a long journey instead of a quick merry-go-round, is a helpful ministry.

Clifford Adams:[5]

> *To think of courtship as romance is natural; to think of marriage as no more than romance is to mistake its reality. For you to embark on marriage seeking a perpetual idyll is to deny its deepest meaning.*

Poetically stated by Matthew Arnold:[6]

> *Who ordered, that their longing's fire*
> *Should be, as soon as kindled, cooled?*
> *Who renders vain their deep desire? —*
> *A God, a God their severance ruled!*

It is the duty (sometimes painful) of the pre-marriage counselor to break through the expectation of perpetual bliss, and help the couple replace that hopeless outlook with a higher vision. To experience God's love and grace through another human being is the greatest gift a couple can give to each other. Unfortunately, through soap operas, magazines, novels, and even the cartoons on which we were brought up, we are taught to believe in the "myth of bliss" (say that five times fast!), rather than a truer, better and even sometimes easier, model.

In the soaps, the deliriously happy are the romantic ones, the ones who are swept away by passionate kissing and dalliances with paramours. The myth of bliss (I like that phrase!) is negatively reinforced by those characters who are portrayed as horribly unhappy, defeated, even suicidal, because marriage is not all it was cracked up to be, that is, anything less than Nirvana. Even the sitcoms do this.

To my mind, one of the worst shows on TV is "Married With Children." Here the husband is bored and annoyed with his wife's sexual advances, the kids are in constant trouble and up to their eyeballs in at-risk behavior, everybody's miserable, and we think it is funny. Why? Because we can identify with the disillusionment. You can't blame the TV and movie industries; they have stumbled upon a pathos that sells. People working out their difficulties, getting comfortable with one another, moving beyond the addiction to the fireworks of romance, and on toward the unlimited energy of "nuclear fusion," is boring! But it is also what we need. (For an excellent overview and critique of cultural views on love and marriage, see Seidenberg, Robert. *Marriage in Life and Literature.* New York. Philosophical Library. 1970.)

Offering this higher vision is the job of the Church. Only the Church has as its mission to break through the cultural myths, and offer Christ. Only the Church has the function of what some have called the "court jester." The jester's job is to criticize the king and queen (or the culture), and to help them see their folly. In the modern folly of weddings and marriage, the Church loses its job as court jester when it is the author, rather than the critic, of such nonsense.

The grinning pastor, allowing any and all forms of sentimentality and dog-and-pony show to invade the rite of the Church, and culminating her/his work with a sloppy sermon on feeling good, and being happy, and keeping a smile on your face, etc. helps not at all. What helps is realistic counseling, and a dignified service. I include planning the wedding as part of marriage preparation. Choosing hymns, scripture readings, etc., can be an excellent opportunity for therapy and teaching, a reminder of the centrality of Christ, and applying the truth of the Gospel to the truth of life together in marriage. Giving the couple a vision of God's love is the greatest gift of ministry we have to offer.

Akin to this is helping the couple see their similarities and contrasts. We often assume that because we have much in common with someone we like, that we have everything in common. In fact, we have led very similar lives in many respects, but each of us is unique, coming from diverse backgrounds and experiences. Knowing where we are alike can help us work for allowing our partner to be genuine. Seeing your own faults and shortcomings can help you accept your partner's. It adds the Christian element of grace.

To the couples intending to get married, in regard to counseling I say, go for it! You have nothing to lose, and everything to gain! Exploring the truth may be a bit frightening, and feel threatening to the security of your relationship, but believe me, it is nothing compared to what happens if issues are left unaddressed!

There are a few good tools available for aiding pre-marriage counselors and clergy in marriage preparation. The best I have encountered is produced by Prepare-Enrich, Inc.[7] They offer training sessions nationwide and include an extensive packet of materials that surround three relationship assessments: Prepare, Prepare-MC, and Enrich. Using computer analysis of 125 questions that the couple answers, Prepare-Enrich, Inc. helps the couple discover relationship strengths and work areas. I have had a lot of success using these tools. Why not avail yourself of resources that can improve your marriage, strengthen your union, and aid in your understanding of what the heck this mysterious person is all about? Don't worry, there will always be plenty of mystery left!

Friedman and others have noted that in a so-called "trial marriage" (living together), very often the couple does not begin to experience their real trials until after they are married and have made that final commitment. Then, up burst the flowers in full bloom that had waited as dormant bulbs beneath the surface. It is his thesis that the behavior patterns that we tend most to respect, both good and bad, are those that have been in the family for generations. We almost cannot help ourselves. Friedman's model for pre-marriage counseling (and any other type, for that matter) is the family systems model put forth especially by Murray Bowen.

My purpose is not to say that weddings are unimportant; exactly the opposite. Weddings are more important than we usually give them credit. Friedman interprets the wedding as one of several critical rites of passage. It marks beginnings and endings. As such, they are extremely emotionally charged. Everything is changing, and because of these changes, there is grief, and a natural resistance to the cause of grief: the change being in this case, the marriage. So it is that parents become over-involved, sisters don't like the dresses they have to wear, whose church, which minister, and on and on go the seemingly trivial conflicts that are actually disguised attempts at sabotage.

On a conscious level, friends and families want things to go smoothly, and wish the couple well in all things. But unconsciously (and therefore, perhaps more genuinely), nearly everyone is grieving the changes that must take place in order for the relationship to work. So the sabotage goes on in an attempt to stop the change and, failing that, to reverse the relationship rather than adjust to it. Example: in-laws take sides with their son/daughter against their new daughter/son-in-law. When everybody takes sides, we are a functioning unit again. If the couple can work out their difficulties, then they are a distinct functioning unit, and the dreaded change is in place (and everyone has to adjust to that). We don't like change, and marriage changes everything. So we get a little crazy when it comes to weddings.

Note to Pastors: I urge you to read Edwin Friedman's book, *Generation to Generation*,[8] especially chapter 7: "A Family Approach to Life-Cycle Ceremonies." He has some truly amazing and extremely helpful insights to offer in understanding and managing the craziness that often surrounds weddings, funerals, baptisms, and so forth.

Chapter Four

Fee? Fee?

Here's a delicate subject: how much to pay the minister performing the ceremony. I suppose that all depends on one's outlook. I personally view weddings as a ministry of the Church, and therefore do not charge a fee, per se. There is a small ($25) administrative fee for the use of the pre-marriage issues-evaluation instrument that I use, but that goes to the company, not to me. Personally, I do not accept gratuities. I figure that the various ministerial tasks of the ordained is what my congregation pays me for, and my salary ought to be sufficient. If not, the solution is not to charge for weddings and funerals, but to talk to my congregation about being underpaid.

In my particular denomination (Lutheran), marriage is not a sacrament, but a rite. Still, I feel that there is something not quite correct about charging for the ritual services of the Church, any more than it is right to offer the sacraments for sale. Ministry simply is not a commercial product.

So what do I do with the gratuities that people give me despite this pronouncement? They go into a church-held account that I can tap at any time for any special need that I see fit to spend it on. This has been a real boon to my ministry for lots of reasons.

First of all, I am able to not feel prostituted. If I don't want to "do a wedding" for whatever reason, I do not feel obligated by some previously agreed-to fee. If Jack and Jill want to get married, and they seem to be perfectly ill-suited for each other, I can opt out. This is much better ministry than Marryin' Buryin' Sam (or Samantha) who will, for a fee, put on a show anytime, anywhere. If you just want to get married in a romantic setting, hire a justice of the peace, and go to the lake, the museum, the botanical garden, or the Brooklyn Bridge!

The wedding in a church building should be a worship service, and specifically, a Christian worship service. I know that is not what people want, but the Church, if it is a business at all, is a single-product enterprise. We are singly about proclaiming the Gospel of Jesus Christ. If we are asked to do anything other than convey that Good News, our response should simply be what President Ronnie thought was the solution to kids taking drugs: "Just say NO!" Refusing a fee makes me feel much freer to protect the Church from being co-opted.

Where my denomination stands on the issue is unclear. (This should be no surprise, as we are only six years old, and are working out a lot of bugs!) But in one of our Previous Church Bodies (PCBs), long before the triumvirate that made up the ELCA, the United Lutheran Church, over 70 years ago, had this to say: "The rite of Christian marriage is a service of the Church and its distinctly religious character should never be subordinated to other considerations."[1]

The Federal Church, of that same era, was even more to the point:

> *"Commercialization of weddings, whether by ministers or civil officials, and degradation of marriage by stunt weddings, by advertising for them, or by using them for advertising purposes, is shocking and antisocial. All of these practices mean that weddings are conducted without sufficient regard for the sacredness of the ceremony, or the spiritual welfare of the persons involved, and they make improbable either the premarital instruction or the later pastoral service which the minister ought to give."*[2]

The other benefit of depositing gratuities in the church's contingency fund (aside from not worrying about tax laws and such) is that I am able to do some extraordinary ministry with that money. When I need a babysitter during a church function, I hire one. When a special charitable cause comes to my attention, and there is no place in the budget for it, I can make a donation. I never worry about this money, and I never miss it. If you are a minister of the Gospel, I highly recommend this program.

Now, as to how much is appropriate if a fee is accepted. In the next chapter entitled, "Inexpensive, Not Cheap!" I cite an article that indicated $166 was the average fee that clergy received for weddings. I have never seen anything close to that, though a friend of mine, (Pastor Dogbreath) received $200 on one occasion. Both of us are worth a whole lot more than that! Take a look at what you get:

•Twelve hours of pre-marriage counseling and wedding planning (on the average). Call any therapist in the telephone book, and see what twelve hours of marriage counseling costs!

•An hour and a half of rehearsal time.

•Three hours of time at the ceremony (including opening up, locking up, pictures, and of course, the ceremony itself).

•At least two hours of sermon preparation time (unless the minister uses one of my sermons in this book!).

•Probably two hours of rehearsal dinner time.

•Probably two hours at the reception (minimum!).

That is twenty-three and a half hours per wedding. At a lump sum of $166, the minister's services come at the bargain rate of $7.06 per hour. As I said earlier, the most frequent amount that I receive for a gratuity is around $50, so that comes out to about $2 an hour. At best, that is pretty poor wages for what we are called to do; at worst, it is an insult! You could make a whole lot more driving a truck, and never work weekends! But then we get back to my original point: this is the ministry of the Church, not a product for sale.

So, if you are reading this book as one who is planning to get married, think about what you are asking your minister to do, and how much that is truly worth. If you are a minister of the Gospel, think about what your real ministry is here, how priceless that is, and don't turn it into a business.

Of late, many of my colleagues have asked this rather interesting question: "How did we ever get ourselves into performing this work for the state?" In other words, marriage per se is not a religious entity, it is a legal arrangement. A woman and a man decide to combine their assets in a binding partnership. This really should not interest the Church whatsoever.

The State in which I live (Wisconsin) has so thoroughly assumed that it is the clergy who are responsible for this function, that it offers a stiff fine and imprisonment if the presider does not file the completed marriage license in a timely fashion! This gets even more ridiculous when you realize that virtually anyone can perform this function! You do not even have to be registered in any official capacity. (This may differ in other states.)

The early Church of the first three centuries after Christ did not consider marriage any particular business of the Church, except in two basic areas. 1) As in all things, in weddings and in the marriage relationship itself, Christians were expected to conduct themselves with decorum and restraint, according to their status as the baptized. That is, act like you are a child of God, for Christ's sake (meant literally, not profanely). Thus, gluttonous feasting, drinking to excess, and orgies were strongly discouraged. 2) In the ritual act of marrying, under no circumstances were the baptized to engage in pagan practices that would lend credence to them. Of special concern were sacrifices to any and all gods.

Local marriage customs were basically the accepted norm (with the above-noted exceptions), and marriages between pagans, as well as between pagans and Christians were honored as valid. (Though evidently Tertullian did not view such marriages as anything but dangerously demonic.) Only very much later did the Church widely move toward considering marriage a sacrament in the more modern sense of the word. Marriages were primarily civil or familial affairs. As the Church grew in prominence and power, this changed somewhat.

Still, well into the fourth century, the role of the clergy was primarily one of blessing a marriage that already existed. The priests were neither functionaries of civil nor ecclesiastical law when it came to weddings. Clergy did not "perform" marriages, nor regulate them, but blessed them with prayer and counsel. The role was pastoral. It was the concern of the Church that Christ be central to the relationship.

By the fifth century, a nuptial mass and the priestly function of blessing a civil or familial marriage contract was in place in some parts of the Roman Church. But by no means was such a priestly function a requirement. According to Schillebeeckx, "During the first ten centuries there was no obligation to receive it."[3]

Not until the roles of the Church and state were thoroughly confused did this situation change. By the time of the Reformation (1516 AD, and following) Europe was dominated by the Roman Church. In the late Middle Ages, both the state and the Church recognized the validity of any marriage as long as there was mutual consent between the man and woman. As political power shifted from the nobility to the Church hierarchy, the Church became not only the guarantors of pastoral care and morality, but we also came to have legal authority in this and many other areas. The propriety of this shift, that is, to ask whether the Church should be doing this, seemingly occurred to no one.

I expect that in the United States we got into the marryin' business not too long ago, when it was simply assumed that mainline Christendom was the dominant religious feature of our culture. "Everybody" belonged to a church, and therefore, "everybody" got married in a church. This popular myth extended so far as to lead to Las Vegas-style wedding chapels, for those in a hurry, or the not-too-religious, but who still felt that if they weren't married in at least something that looked like a church, then well, they just weren't married!

Time for a revolution! The plain truth is that only about 40 percent of all U.S. citizens are affiliated with an established religious group, and that includes non-Christian religions. Time to give back the legal function to its proper owner, the state. If members of the Church want to be married, and theologically we can support the institution of marriage, that is fine. If offering a wedding service is a useful "in" for initiating new members into the Body of Christ, or retrieving "lost sheep," great! But for those who are just wanting to rent the hall because it is pretty, send 'em packin'! The Christian minister has better things to do with her or his time, like preach the Gospel.

Of course, you can use these occasions for a crack at witnessing to the unbelievers — not only the couple, but all their guests. So maybe you don't want to slam the door in their faces, but neither do you want to leave the door wide open for vandals to destroy your true treasure: Jesus Christ.

It is for this reason that I have developed a counseling contract which I share with you at the end of this chapter. As long as you give appropriate credit, or at least not claim it as your own and make big bucks off of it, you may use it word for word.

A few comments on this might be called for. I use this contract for members and non-members alike. It serves the function of telling the couples I am working with that I take my role as a minister very seriously, and I expect them to take this pre-marriage counseling very seriously, too. The entire purpose of this agreement is to do everything we can to invest a whole lot more in the marriage than in the wedding.

I no longer stipulate the item on tithing. Pity. It is probably the most important aspect of the contract! Tithing has a way of giving a gift to the tither that can only be experienced. I believe it can only enhance a relationship if the couple discovers the joy of making that kind of real commitment to God's work in the Church. Unfortunately, more than one couple groused at even trying the Biblical imperative. Some simply refused to do it. Since I usually had no way of checking that anyway, the relationship with me was less than honest, thus defeating the purpose of the item to begin with (that is, to discover the joy of tithing). Finally, my mutual ministry committee insisted that I remove it, and reluctantly, I dropped it.

Weekly worship attendance is the second most important item in the contract. I like this one (and the tithing) especially when I work with couples of two different denominations or faiths. A couple that can share spiritual values, and even appreciate spiritual contrasts between them, will certainly have a strength in their relationship that cannot be found elsewhere. So I encourage the couple to worship together. If that means going to two services each week, or alternating between their two traditions, great! The point is the sharing.

The alcohol and other drug abuse (AODA) stipulations are simple pragmatism. The single most common and most severe factor in failing relationships is, without a doubt, alcohol and other drug abuse and/or other addictions. I almost never encounter a couple or a family that is experiencing difficulties that is not either directly or indirectly affected by this disease. So, *now*, before the wedding, is the time to discover and address it, not later.

The counselor and the couple are simply wasting their time trying to work on the relationship, if one of them is under the influence of a mood-altering substance. For the addicted person, this is doubly so. If one of the parties has experienced a problem in this area, both should find out what that means in this relationship that they are building. So, for instance, if the man used to have (or still has) a problem with any substance, then he should go to AA, NA, SAA, or whatever is appropriate, and the woman should go to Al-Anon. He has to get a handle on his problem (himself and the substance), and she has to get a handle on her problem (herself and him)! (And vice-versa, of course, if the woman is addicted, and the man is co-dependent.) If they don't, they are in for misery. There is a lot of literature on this subject, almost everywhere you turn.

I use the term "substance abuse" because it is so broad. This includes, for some, food, and for still others, sex. The basic dynamics are much the same, in any case.

Why am I so direct and uncompromising in these matters? Well, as I said before, I'm interested primarily in ministry. If I can help a couple see and address their issues, then I have done my job. If I can help them overcome their difficulties and build a new life together that is founded in Christian love, then I have been privileged to be the instrument of a miraculous healing! I feel no less delighted when a couple decides not to get married as a result of our work together, than when a couple is happily married. Marriage is hard work. Why should weddings be easy?

Counseling Contract For Couples
Page 1

In entering into a counseling relationship with Pastor *(insert name here)* _____, we agree to the following conditions while working with her (him):

1. We will attend worship together on a weekly basis; our own congregation, or another, whatever best suits our spiritual needs.

2. We will tithe (give 10%) of our income to whatever congregation we attend.

3. If either of us are involved or have been involved in any form of substance abuse, we will attend a 12-Step support group (whichever is appropriate) on a weekly basis.

4. If either of us are involved or have been involved in any form of substance abuse, we agree to abstain from all mood-altering substances.

5. We will regularly keep our appointments with Pastor *(insert name here)* _____, and will try our best to apply to our lives what we have learned.

6. We will contact Pastor *(insert name here)* _____ if and when a crisis arises.

_____   _____
           (signed)   *(date)*

_____   _____
           (signed)   *(date)*

Counseling Contract For Couples
Page 2

I, *(insert name here)* _____, Pastor, will, in helping the signees:

1. Keep confidential all information pertaining to them except when it would place them or others in danger.

2. Keep all appointments except in an emergency.

3. Be prepared in all ways possible in advance of appointments.

4. Help to the best of my ability, with the concerns we discuss.

5. Refer them to another helping professional when appropriate.

6. Agree that they may call me at any time when a crisis arises.
Office Phone _____ Home Phone _____

_____   _____
(signed)   *(date)*

Chapter Five

Inexpensive, Not Cheap

Where I presently live, people go nuts spending money on their weddings. And then they skimp on their honeymoon, or miss a house payment, or their parents have to take out a second mortgage. You do not have to do this to yourself in order to have a very fine wedding.

"Hello, Fancy Schmancy Hotel? I'd like to rent one of your reception rooms for my wedding."

"Of course. And how many guests would you like to have?"

"Oh, about 300."

"I see. I assume you would like to do this on a Saturday evening?"

"Of course!"

"We have January 6th of next year available."

"Oh ... I was hoping to get something in the summer. Preferably June."

"I see." (There is a long pause, and you swear you hear someone desperately choking back laughter.) "Let me just check." (An even longer pause.) "Hello, Ma'am?"

"Yes?"

"Two thousand thirty-five."

"Gee, that's a lot less than I expected for 300 people! That's not bad at all!"

"Uh, Ma'am?"

"Yes?"

"That's not the price of the hall."

"Oh?"

"No Ma'am. 2035 is the next year we have an opening on a Saturday in June."

Doubtless the single most expensive item, that is very traditional around here, is the reception. And it is the most limiting factor in determining when the wedding will take place.

Everybody wants the Fancy Schmancy Hotel Downtown for the reception, so when the hotel says they have an opening on Saturday January 6th, that's when you have your wedding. Then you check with everybody else to see how that fits with their schedule. I don't know how many times I've had a phone conversation with someone looking for a preacher whose schedule matches up with when the Fancy Schmancy Hotel Downtown said they could get married. And frankly, I just can't figure out the big attraction. They always serve the same over-priced, greasy chicken, and over-cooked roast beef, and they have lousy mashed potatoes!

So, before you launch headlong into something that could turn out to be receivership, let's think this through more completely. Is the Hotel Fancy Schmancy really necessary? I've been to some mighty nice receptions at lesser-priced joints. How about the party house at your apartment complex? You know, the one with the swimming pool. Depending on the type of party you throw, you may yourself end up being thrown in the pool, but who says it has to be out of control? And if you want an informal, fun-filled bash, what more appropriate place? Just doff your rented formal wear before you show up!

Or, have you thought of renting a large, circus-type tent, and having the reception in your backyard, or at a friend's farm? What about a picnic shelter in the park? These can be very inexpensive receptions, and truly wonderful, family gatherings. Of course, this assumes a wedding during the warmer months. I used to live in a community where the local Lion's Club rented a very nice tent for an extremely reasonable fee; included in the price was erecting and striking the tent. Call around; shop! It may prove worth your while.

Then there are the less expensive bars and restaurants which would love to close down and go private for a few hours. Some would be just great for moderate-sized gatherings. But don't overlook your best bet yet: the church fellowship hall.

Most churches charge a nominal cleaning fee, and that is about it. Many congregations charge nothing if you are a member. Just clean up after yourselves, and have a good time. More and more congregations have no smoking and no alcoholic beverages (other than communion wine) policies, and these restrictions may influence your decision. But, hey, you can have a good time without smoke and booze, can't you? Maybe not.

Going with these alternatives may mean a little more work for a lot less money. Here is the secret to a little more work: every one of your closest friends is dying to help with the wedding! Ask Kathi and Jim to help set up the tables and chairs, and Alex and Jessica and Kelly and Rosie to help with cleanup. Arlene and Beth would love nothing more than to cater this whole thing, and Michael really enjoys flower arranging . . . and so on. Get the picture? At our wedding, Neal got most of the pictures. And you know what? They turned out a lot better than those hokey, professionally-posed jobs. Neal just wandered around, taking candid photos, and discreetly captured the spirit of the occasion. Of course, afterward we took a few posed shots, but frankly, they are not the ones we really treasure. Thank you, Neal!

What a gift Neal gave us, too! According to an AP article printed in my local newspaper on April 21, 1991, the average traditional wedding costs a whopping $16,000! For better or for broke! Of that, the average photographer's fee was $908. A local photographer, trying to capitalize and compete, advertises that you will not pay that much using their service, no siree! "Our package starts at $499.99, and you always keep the negatives!" That's right, a lot of the photographers sell you prints only. If you want more prints, you must go through them to get them made up, and if you somehow bypass that, you are in danger of violating copyright laws! All for a mere $908! Doubtless, Neal gave us our most expensive wedding gift, and had a lot of fun doing it.

Not only does this not have to be one giant pain between the ears, and deplete your life savings, your friends and family would very much appreciate the opportunity to contribute to your happy occasion. They want to feel a part of your joy, so let them! Ask them!

(A few personal notes of thanks: Dad and Mom, thanks for the cream puffs and the chicken, brats, and corn on the cob and the keg. And to my acquired parents, thanks for the strawberries, shortcake, whipped cream, etc. Deb, Elaine, Louise, thanks for serving the punch, champagne and eats. And Hank and Shirla, thank you for baking the marvelous wedding bread that we used for Holy Communion.)

———————

Here is what just one department store (years ago) offered in one typical Midwestern American city.[1] They published their own, rather extensive wedding planning book, surely in the hopes of getting you to shop there for all of your wedding "needs." The frontispiece and the introduction, clearly were commercials aimed at the bride. (After all, everyone knows that the groom makes no plans at all for the wedding, except to show up with his hair combed, fingernails cleaned, and preferably sober.) Here is an age-old "joke" you may have heard: "The wedding is for the bride; the honeymoon is for the groom." (Gag me.)

So, this department store had:

"Special Services for the Bride"

The Bride's Shop, featuring wedding gowns, veils, attendant's attire — Third Floor

Candice Kane (a real sweetheart), Consultant, Bride's Shop, Wedding Portraits, and Candids of Weddings, Special Bridal Photo Studio — Third Floor

Arlene Skoor, Gift Registry — Fifth Floor

Engraved Invitations, and Other Stationery Needs — First Floor

Wedding Cakes to Order, in the Bake Shop — First Floor

Jimi Hendrix Travel Bureau — Annex

Interior Decorating Studios — Fourth Floor

And of course, Credit Offices — Fourth Floor

(You'd better believe you'll be seeing these folks!)

As if this were not enough:

"Other Services That Will Interest You"

Beauty Salon — Second Floor
Draperies — Fourth Floor
Furniture, Carpets, Linens and Beddings — Fifth Floor
Housewares and Home Appliances — Annex
Better Apparel Shops — Third Floor
Lamps, Pictures, Mirrors — Fifth Floor
Budget Apparel Shops — Second Floor
Lingerie, Foundation Garments — Second and Third
   Floors (!)
Collegianne Shops — Third Floor
Luggage — Annex
Diamonds, and Other Fine Jewelry — First Floor
Negligees and Robes — Third Floor (more undies!?)
Fashion Accessory Shops — First Floor
Silverware, China, Glass — Fifth Floor

I think it is just great that we have all these wonderful things to choose from! I really do, but as Tony Campolo says, "*Wake Up America*!"[2] These things will not make you happy, much less fulfill the deepest desires of your soul. There is, however, an entire industry hoping to convince you that their things can and will do just that. Happiness is for sale, and if you cannot afford it now, why wait for bliss? Please see the friendly people in the credit department!

The title line of the foreword of this wedding planning book, (a.k.a. sales pitch)? "For the Happiest Time of Your Life." Right. As my good friend, Pastor Dogbreath says, "I haven't seen a lot of happy wedding parties ... I have seen a lot of exhausted ones!"

But not one to leave a dead horse unwhipped, I press on. The bride is encouraged to "Love every minute of being the center of attention ... and accept with gracious enthusiasm all the expressions of devotion and interest your family, friends and acquaintances heap upon you." (Not to mention all the gifts!)

75

Please, dear brides, resist the temptation to let anyone make you queen for a day! It will do you no good, and is likely to put a barrier between you and your friends, and very possibly your family, in-laws, and even your intended spouse. The queen in any setting is lonely; she has few friends, many courtiers, but no peers.

The focus in a Christian wedding, and hopefully, the marriage that follows, is not the bride, not even (more egalitarian) the bride and groom; it is Christ. Jesus Christ is the center of our lives. This we can celebrate with just as much joy and enthusiasm as anything our culture can cook up. Our culture offers the wedding couple, or more likely, the bride, at best a few moments in the spotlight, usually at an exorbitant price. Jesus Christ offers us New Life, even in our marriages, and completely at His expense! What a deal!

Celebration is certainly called for, but always, as the Presbyterians remind us, "with decency and in good order." As the pastor, I have very little input in the reception aspect of the day. But at the church wedding, I am in charge. I tell the wedding party that I will not tolerate drunkenness at the wedding, and if anyone shows up drunk, including the bride and groom, they will be asked to leave. If that means no wedding, then that's what it means. The last thing I want to do is officiate over the union of two persons, one of whom was under the influence at the time! In fact, in many states it is illegal to do so.

The reception is another matter. Personally, I like a glass of bubbly, or a cocktail before or with dinner, but I am never disappointed if none is offered. In fact, the very best reception I have been to was Lisa Woods' and Mason Chang's, at which sparkling grape juice was served. It was a delightful afternoon, and the prevailing mood was peace and joy. It was a pleasure to be part of their wedding!

I have already cited Elizabeth Swadley's book. Though her work is somewhat dated, she still said some things occasionally that had merit. Her declaration regarding alcoholic beverages however, is extremist and ill-founded (that is, basically, that alcohol invites the devil to your wedding). But I agree with her in at least this: the wedding reception should never be an occasion for even one guest to get drunk. The bride and groom will ruin their wedding entirely if either of them is inebriated. A glass or two of champagne is fine, but never go overboard. Nothing is more disturbing than a drunken bride or groom, or worse, someone passing out, vomiting, or getting in a fight because of booze. Avoid the probability by serving controlled and moderate amounts. Avoid the possibility entirely by serving non-alcoholic beverages.

If you do not have a lot of money to spend, you may welcome the permission to opt out of this destructive and expensive enterprise. Hopefully, you are beginning to see that you can have a marvelous wedding without being shackled with inordinate debt, filing bankruptcy, or murdering your rich uncle. If, however, money is no object (and you are still reading this book!), you may be wondering, "What's the big deal?"

There is a lot to the big deal, actually. First, no matter how much money you have, assuming that you are a person of faith, squandering what God has given you is sin. It is bad stewardship. The Lord gave you all that you have, not with the idea that you would waste your gifts in meaningless trimmings, but that you would glorify God with your life. As with all gifts, the greater the gift, the greater the responsibility. I do not know who said this first: "God gives gifts not for privilege, but for purpose." If you've been lavishly gifted in this life, the Lord has given you the power to do some great things. The only privilege that you have been given is more purposeful living.

Recently I heard a radio advertisement so considerately advising the listener on how much to spend on an engagement ring. The guideline? Six months' salary! No one has the right to spend that kind of proportion on their jewelry. It is an indecent and immoral excess. When will we learn that it is not the accumulation of things, much less being a slave to our possessions, that will buy us happiness? Joy is not to be found in riches!

What you can spend on wedding dresses, formal wear, flowers, cake, refreshments, entertainment, and reception is obscene. It is neither necessary, nor, in many cases, right. Do yourself, your family and friends, and society a favor: rebel! Opt out! Do your own thing! It will not only be cheaper, but very possibly, far more meaningful.

"Well, if I don't spend heaps of money on my wedding, what shall I do with all the wealth that I am saving?" How about saving some of it? How about a downpayment on a house, or going on a truly great honeymoon? Better still, how about giving it away? This may be the most strident statement in this book, but nothing will be a more important investment in your marriage than the money that you give away!

My friend, Glen Holmquist, likes to advise the 10-10-80 plan. You save 10 percent, you give 10 percent to God, who gave it all to you in the first place, and you live on 80 percent. The blessings of that kind of disciplined lifestyle, and the freedom that comes from that kind of discipline, must be experienced to be believed. You can do it! There are billions of people on this planet who would just love to have the opportunity to make it on 80 percent of what you have. They are better managers (stewards) than you and me. I'm not talking about the masses of human beings that live in squalor and at the edge of starvation, but of the vast majority of people who are doing more than just existing on far less than what you have at your disposal.

The problems are outlook and priorities. We believe that everything we have is necessary. This is not true. Our priorities place the accumulation of comforts over that which has true worth, such as our relationships, the good of our fellow human beings, and the tiny biosphere in which we all must live. How we spend what God has given us has a direct bearing on all of this, and more.

Try tithing! You will be amazed at the difference it makes in your life. It will not fix everything that is wrong with the world (though it will help a great deal), nor will it be the key to the happiness for which you have been so desperately searching. It will not, as some maintain, make you more successful in your business by raising profits 1,000 percent. But it will be a significant way of choosing to live life in a way that God promises will be rewarding in the extreme. It will prioritize your life in a way that is not "of this world," but merely "in it." Just try it. I have never met a former tither!

Chapter Six

Presents Or Presence?

"No, Hairball! You miss the point! You don't invite people you want to show up at your wedding, you invite people who will give you the best presents!" So went the advice of one of my very best friends and colleagues at the occasion of my wedding. He was half-serious! But then, this low-life, gravy-sucking pig has always had a "thing about things!"

The Adventures of Shock Trousseau

The history of the trousseau is very easily traced to what used to be called the "hope chest," and this traced to the "dowry," and this to brides for purchase, and theft![1] Where once the bride was stolen, and then perhaps paid for, the arrangement of marriages by purchase of the bride took over as the more "civilized" way. Shortly following the purchase of brides comes the interesting inversion of the bride accumulating some wealth of her own, to make the deal more attractive to prospective mates. The man paid the father of the bride the "wed," or a "troth" (a promise of paying such a wed) (cf. Chapter 1 "Customary, But Stupid!"), and he was eager to do so, if the dowry, or hope chest was sufficiently full of good stuff. It was the custom in many places for the mother of the groom to come and inspect the hope chest.

Accumulating important items for setting up a new household can be very helpful, but a dowry, and/or a hope chest, is an outdated and unnecessary custom. Not only are brides no longer for sale (thank God!), but couples starting a new life together are rarely starting from scratch. The custom of publishing a list of what gifts you would like for your trousseau seems a bit abusive of your invited guests, and is buying heavily into what the wedding industry dictates you should do.

Of course, it is in their best interests if you publish your wish list, linen preference, or silver and china patterns with their company!

Many wedding books will tell you what they think you should include in your published trousseau. I'm not going to![2] If your friends know you, they may already be aware of what you need and don't need. And if they ask, maybe you would want to have a list of helpful suggestions, but how much fun is that? Why don't you let them decide how to express their love to you? They might come up with much better ideas, and much more personally derived and meaningful gifts that you will cherish, rather than that silver butter dish that you have just been dying to get your hands on.

Contrary to what my friend Michael says, the reason you are inviting these people is not to accumulate wealth, but to have the people that mean much to you present for your send-off into marriage. I have always appreciated the invitations that say, "Please come! We want your presence, not your presents!" If I had to choose between a friend or family member paying for a flight, bus ticket, or a motel room, as opposed to buying me a gift of equal value, I'd pick the person being there with me, every time!

Appendix A

A Sample
Parish Wedding Policy Booklet

Each congregation should have a printed wedding policy handbook. This will save the ministers of worship, music, pastoral care, and others, much grief and headache. This type of document should be constructed with the help of the organist, sexton, janitor, pastor, secretary, altar guild, and all others in the church who are directly affected by wedding ministries. It should be easy to understand, and as one professor of mine was fond of saying (and we were fond of mimicking), "terse, pithy, and succinct."

Your Wedding At
Gloria Dei Lutheran Church
Neenah, Wisconsin

Introduction

Congratulations on your engagement to be married! We of Gloria Dei Lutheran Church are pleased to be able to minister to your special needs as you prepare to be married. We hope this booklet and associated materials in this packet will be helpful to you now and in the years to come.

Preliminary Decisions

1. **The Wedding Date.** As soon as you can, contact the pastor to establish the date of your wedding. The pastor will try to accommodate you, but the later you make these arrangements, the more likely scheduling conflicts will arise. A date and time for rehearsal will need to be established as well. Traditionally, weddings are not celebrated during Holy Week.

2. Pre-Marital Counseling. The pastor will not preside at a wedding which has not had adequate planning and preparation. Our hope for you is that you will be preparing for your marriage as well as your wedding, therefore pre-marriage counseling is a must. This ministry to you takes an investment of time. So again, early contact with the pastor is essential. There may be a nominal administrative fee for the use of an inventory instrument, such as *Prepare*.

3. Organist, Music. If organ music is desired, early contact with the organist is also advisable. The Church organist should be your first option out of courtesy to that person's position in the church. The pastor and organist will be glad to help you select music that is appropriate to the Christian worship setting. The final approval of all music at the wedding rests with the pastor and the organist.

The Marriage Service

Marriage is a service of worship in which the invited guests are not mere spectators but participants in the service. They are not there simply to watch, but to be a congregation of God's people. The pastor will discuss with you the nature and form of the marriage service. The service beginning on page 202 of the *Lutheran Book of Worship* provides an excellent reference for the pastor and you in planning your special worship service.

You are encouraged to consider celebrating Holy Communion as a service of worship, surrounding your wedding ceremony. The liturgy of Holy Communion stresses several important themes: The centrality of Christ in your relationship, the Love of God, unity, forgiveness. The wedding couple can play a special part in this worship service.

Readings from Scripture are an important aspect of every Christian wedding. Your selection is unlimited, however, the following are readings that many couples have found meaningful. We suggest you read each of these together (perhaps one a day as a daily devotional) and pick those which you find most meaningful to your relationship. It is traditional (though not required) that you select 3 readings: Old Testament, New Testament, and a Gospel lesson, and perhaps a Psalm to be read or sung as well.

Suggested Readings

Psalms: 33, 100, 117, 127, 128, 136, 150

Old Testament:
Genesis 1:26-31
Genesis 2:18-24 (include
  vs. 25?)
Ruth 1:16-17
Song of Solomon (Song of
  Songs) 2:10-17 (omit vs. 15?)
Song Of Solomon 8:7
Isaiah 60:19-22
Isaiah 63:7-9

Gospel Lessons:
Matthew 19:3-6
Matthew 22:34-40
Mark 10:2-9
John 2:1-10
John 15:9-12
John 17:11, 15-19

New Testament:
Romans 12:1-3, 9-13
1 Corinthians 12:31-13:13
  (or a portion thereof)
Galatians 5:22-26
Ephesians 5:21-33
Philippians 1:27-2:5
Philippians 4:4-7 (8-9)
Colossians 2:6-7
Colossians 3:12-17
Hebrews 13:1-6
1 Peter 1:13-16, 22-25
1 Peter 3:8-9
2 Peter 1:3-11
2 Peter 3:11-15a
1 John 2:12-17
1 John 3:18-24
1 John 4:7-12

The Wedding Rehearsal

The wedding rehearsal is important so that everything will be done, as scripture says, "decently and in order" during the service.

Please be on time for the rehearsal! See that all the participants are present. These include the couple, the best man, maid/matron of honor, the bridesmaids, groomsmen, ushers, parents, readers, acolytes, and organist.

Special arrangements should be made for the soloist to meet and practice with the organist.

If you will be rearranging the furniture in the worship area (eg: making a center aisle) you will want to arrive early to do this so that we may begin the rehearsal on time. Please note that at the conclusion of your wedding, you must see to it that the worship area is returned to its original arrangement.

Notes Concerning The Service

The Christian Wedding Service is a joyous and happy occasion. However, the conduct of all participants should be in keeping with the solemnity of the service. The Pastor reserves the right to halt any service when a member of the party or any guests in the church are not conducting themselves with propriety.

All decorations, aisle runner, and wedding candle (if used) are to be provided by the bridal party. The placement of decorations should be cleared with the pastor. Candelabra are furnished by the church if you want to use them. (See page 86-87 for the schedule of fees.)

Arrangements for bulletins may be made with the pastor.

No flash pictures shall be taken during the service. Please ask your photographer to check with the pastor before the service. Pictures are usually taken after the service and receiving line, but you may find it more convenient to take pictures before the service.

The throwing of rice is inappropriate to our Christian setting (actually, this is a Buddhist fertility rite). It is messy, and some have suggested that it actually is harmful to birds that may eat the rice left on the ground. For these reasons, we ask that you not throw rice.

Rentals And Fees

Suggested honoraria:

Soloist	$30.00
Organist	$50.00
•Pastor	$50.00

•Many pastors do not accept honoraria for weddings as they consider this a ministry of the Church for which they are already paid. The pastor may donate this money to special uses in the Church.

Fees:

> Fellowship Hall and Kitchen $25.00
> (non-members)
> Candles $15.00
> (for candelabras and aisle candles)

Gloria Dei has no custodian. If the facilities need to be cleaned or pews put back in order, this is your responsibility. If you desire other arrangements for cleaning the facilities you may make them with the pastor.

Receptions

You are welcome to use our Fellowship Hall for your reception. You are reminded that caterers do not set up or clean up, and you are responsible for seeing that this gets done. Parties using the facilities are responsible for all damage and breakage. If you desire the pastor to attend special dinners or receptions, please remember to send an invitation.

Alcohol

The use of alcoholic beverages is prohibited at the church or on the grounds with the exception of wine for communion.

Smoking

Smoking is prohibited in all areas indoors. Please ask your guests to respect this rule and to smoke only out of doors if they must smoke.

Wedding Music

Since the marriage celebration is a worship service, the music should be chosen carefully, with discrimination, and in consultation with the pastor and organist. The instrumental and vocal music should not be thought of as entertainment or background music, but rather as music of praise to God for the inspiration of all those who are present. Therefore, extreme care should be taken in choosing both the soloist and the music.

It is most appropriate to use congregational hymns during the marriage service. For instance, a hymn might be played on the organ for the wedding processional, with the congregation joining in immediately after the wedding party has arrived at the front of the sanctuary. There are also other appropriate places in the wedding service for congregational singing. Here are few suggestions:

	LBW Hymn Number
The King of Love My Shepherd Is	#456
Love Divine, All Loves Excelling	#315
O Perfect Love	#287
O Holy Spirit, Enter In	#459
Beautiful Savior	#518
Praise, My Soul, The King of Heaven	#549
The Lord's My Shepherd	#451
Lord Jesus Christ, Be Present Now	#253
All People That On Earth Do Dwell	#245
Praise to the Lord, the Almighty	#543
Children of the Heavenly Father	#474
Now Thank We All Our God	#534
Oh, Worship The King	#548
Savior, Like A Shepherd Lead Us	#481
I Will Sing the Story of Your Love	# 16
Let All Things Now Living	#557
Sent Forth By God's Blessing	#221

If you do not wish to use a hymn as part of the processional or recessional, there is a great deal of other music which would be suitable for that purpose. The organist would be happy to help you in making a selection.

Vocal Music

It has become a well established custom to enhance the wedding service through the medium of vocal solos. A great deal of music has found its way into the wedding service which, due to both the words and the music, fails to reinforce the spiritual significance of the wedding service. The wedding service seeks to leave the worshipper touched by the spiritual emphasis which such a service, and the music associated with it, should provide.

Some music may not be appropriate for a church service. You may wish to reserve these selections for the reception.

A folder of appropriate wedding music is available at the church.

A Final Word

It has already been suggested that you use the selected list of readings as a daily devotional as you prepare for your wedding. Additionally, we ask that you attend worship together on a weekly basis, and begin tithing as a spiritual discipline in preparation for your life together.

A well-planned marriage service is a positive beginning for a truly happy and satisfying life together. We encourage you to discuss and plan carefully and seriously. May your special worship service be a great blessing to all who attend.

Appendix B

A Pastor's Wedding Planning Sheet

Page 1

Couple's Names _____   _____

Woman's telephone: _____   _____
                         (home)   *(office)*

Man's telephone: _____   _____
                        (home)   *(office)*

Date of first session _____

Wedding Date _____ Time _____ p.m./a.m.

Rehearsal Date _____ Time _____ p.m./a.m.

Is pastor expected to attend rehearsal dinner? _____

                                          reception? _____

Check List: *(date given)*

Counseling Contract _____ Signed? _____

Church Policy Booklet_____

Planning Booklet _____

Marriage inventory administered _____

90

A Pastor's Wedding Planning Sheet

Page 2

Scriptures chosen _____

_____

_____

Psalm? _____ To be sung or read? _____

Music reviewed by Pastor/Minister of Music? _____

Music chosen _____

_____

_____

_____

_____

Organist contacted? _____

Bulletin cover chosen (catalog #) _____

Bulletin written _____ Bulletin to typist _____

Date counseling completed _____

Notes:

Appendix C

Sermons You Can Use

It is the simple and profound obligation of the preacher to always and without exception, preach Christ and His Gospel. This is a particular challenge when those gathered before you are not expecting this, and even more importantly, are probably not wanting this, either. Mostly, the congregation before you is looking for sentiment and brevity. But, as one teacher of preachers always said, "The text and the occasion may not have the Gospel in it. Your job is to drag it in there anyhow!" Thank you, Dr. Harms, for your evangelical zeal!

Luther[1] wrote in his marriage sermon, first published in 1536, " . . . it is indeed one of the most necessary things in Christendom to preach about, and all Christians should have knowledge of it." The occasion of a wedding is not the only time one should preach about marriage, but it is obviously an opportune time. Everyone's mind is on the subject, and the preacher is likely to be able to preach to some folks that s/he has never seen before, and is unlikely to see again! That preaching is optional in the rite of marriage does not mean that it is unimportant.

Wedding sermons can be either generic, or personal. Mine tend to be personal. Only rarely will I speak on a subject, rather than address a particular couple, or family. There are, however, some recurring themes found in many relationships. For this reason, I have included here a few personal sermons, with introductions that describe specific relational situations. As I have indicated in the preface of this book, names have been changed in all instances except in the following. The first sermon, therefore, is presented without comment.

Tina And Scoot
August 10, 1991
Emmanuel Lutheran Church
Rhinelander, Wisconsin

What does it mean to say, "I love you?" People say those three words all the time, and yet they mean different things to different people. On TV we probably get as good a picture as you are going to get of what is commonly meant by that phrase. On the soap operas, "I love you" frequently means, "Let's go to bed."

Sometimes, "I love you" means, "You're fun to be with" or "You did something that really makes me happy." I remember one movie: the chips were down, and one good guy sees another good guy secretly pulling out a gun, and he says to her, "I love you!" Bumper stickers express this kind of love: "I heart New York" or, "Virginia is for Lovers." Personally, I love ice cream. But I have no intention of marrying ice cream, horses, or fishing.

So what does it mean to say "I love you" in this setting, in a Church wedding? I emphasize the word Church, because A) that's where we are, and B) this is where Tina and Scoot wanted to have this important event in their lives take place. They did not want just a cute or romantic place, they wanted a sacred place to speak of their love for each other.

In the Church, we mean something altogether different when we speak of love. Oh, we feel okay about the other types of love. We rejoice in the gifts of sexual love, and are happy that God gave us the love of ice cream and fishing, and so on. (At least I am thankful for these things, I don't know about you.) But there is a greater love, Christian love, that is altogether different.

Christian love is the gift that God gives us which goes beyond mere feelings. Sexual love, for instance, fades pretty fast. Sometimes, it is only a momentary feeling. Sometimes, sexual love goes dormant. On the other hand, our sexual love may not be part of our conscious thought at all, and suddenly, we

93

see ourselves behaving in a way that is highly motivated sexually. This can be a wonderful feeling, and it can be a terrifying feeling. But whatever quality it has, it is still just a feeling. We don't have much control over our feelings. For good or for ill, feelings are just there. You feel them, or you don't. Action is another matter.

God's love, Christian love, is a decision to act, and not a feeling. We don't know what God feels. God may be angry, or sad, or happy, or jealous, (the writers of the Bible attribute all these feelings to God), but regardless of how God feels, God always loves us. God always chooses to do the loving thing.

Of course, the place we learn this about God is in the person Jesus of Nazareth, the Christ. He is God in the flesh. Jesus showed us how to love beyond how we feel. In Jesus, God felt many things, but loved us ultimately in action. The epitome of this love-in-action, was His death on the cross. We kill Jesus, and what do we get? Love. Forgiveness.

It is in the name of this God that we gather, and it is in this spirit of unconditional love that we in the Church marry. Tina and Scoot have lots of feelings for each other. They like each other. They have fun together. They love many of the same people: family and friends. And they love each other sexually. But they pledge themselves to a radically different, and specifically Christian, way of loving.

Here in the Church, they pledge themselves to God's faithful way of loving. Regardless of how they feel — angry, sad, happy, tired, sexy, dumpy, or nothing at all, — they pledge that they will choose to love each other unconditionally. They pledge to be faithful. Regardless of how they feel, this is how they will act. And, what's more, they promise to do something that they can do only under the power of the Holy Spirit. They promise to forgive, which is the ultimate act of love.

When Tina and Scoot fail to love as faithfully as they might have pledged, they promise to forgive each other. When they break the promises they make today, they will repair that break with forgiveness. This they will do not on their own power, but by the power of God's Holy Spirit.

This is not something that comes naturally. This kind of love is strictly learned behavior. God teaches it through the Church. And that is where we come in. You and I are here to offer Tina and Scoot help and support for this relationship. We, too, make pledges. We will pray for them. We will be there for them when they need us, as will the whole Church of Jesus Christ. And of course, we ask them to be here in the Church for us.

So, we gather in this church building to remind the bride and groom, and to remind ourselves, just what it is we are up to today. We are here to set to the work of Christian love.

Amen

Jessica And Alex
Big Fish, Little Fish Merger
Mark 10:6-9

What happens in a marriage when one person does not respect the other? In this instance, I was very concerned for the couple. The one's ego was so overdeveloped, and coming from such a sense of insecurity, that the other's position in the relationship was, to say the least, sub-standard. Often, I do not choose the scriptures for a wedding. Usually I assign this as an exercise during pre-marriage counseling and wedding preparations. This time, they wanted me to do the choosing. I couldn't pass up the opportunity to get in a last word.

"So that they are no longer two, but one flesh." But obviously we still have two people. What does this oneness mean? It is important not to get so lost in a marriage that one person or the other disappears, gets swallowed up. That is the difference between a merger and a partnership.

In a merger, the big fish swallows the little fish. The two shall become one fish! Marriage is not a merger, but a partnership. Two fish, equal in importance, learn to swim together for their mutual benefit.

Fish do that extremely well. If you have ever watched a school of fish swimming, it is fascinating how they make sudden movements as if they were a single organism, and they never collide! How do they do it? By a peculiar thing called a ventral nerve.

Running along the side of almost all fish is a nerve that is very near the surface of the skin. You can see it with the naked eye. That nerve is sensitive to the movement of everything around. When one fish in the school moves, every other fish feels that movement and responds. It is a very real connection between the fish. Fish in a school no longer act independently as much as inter-actively.

Each fish remains unique. Each fish has its own identity. But each fish is of a greater unit. The school is one flesh. And

96

it is a great adaptation for survival. Responding and corresponding, instead of just two eyes watching out, the school may have hundreds of eyes watching. Together, life is more full, safer, and one could even say better, than it would be individually.

Enough about fish. Alex and Jessica are getting married. They become one. They come, not to merge, with one person taking over the life of the other, absorbing the other, eliminating the other. They come together to combine resources and become a partnership. They come to give the gifts that God has given them to each other, so that together, they may live life more fully.

The reason for any partnership is this: we have enough in common to find a mutual interest, and we have enough differences that we will benefit from each other's gifts. Men and women have much in common, and they have much in contrast. It is really the contrasts that will be the most important. Jessica and Alex are no exception.

Use your differences to complement each other. You each have strengths, and you each have weaknesses. Discover your weaknesses, and let your partner teach you how to do better in that area. Discover your strengths, and share them with your partner. In other words, build a partnership that is based in the desire to be improved.

Now you can only do that if the partnership is based on mutual respect. You recognize that your partner has much to offer. You also need mutual acceptance. You recognize that your partner has flaws, but you accept that as part of the person you are marrying. And that is love that you can promise.

Love necessarily includes a desire to be better than you are today. That is love for yourself as well as your partner. Mutual respect and acceptance are necessary ingredients in a recipe for love. And all three of these aspects of love — the desire to be bettered, respect and acceptance — are exactly what Christ's love is about.

Christ loves us enough to seek our betterment, and therefore offers us himself, gives himself to us, for our good. Christ respects us. He does not force God's love upon us, rather, He respects our integrity, while at the same time offering His unique gifts. And Christ accepts us. Christ does not insist that we change and improve before He loves us. Rather, Christ accepts us just as we are, and offers us love and forgiveness in the hope that we will respond, in the hope that we will become one with God; that we will form a partnership.

May you in your marriage experience the love of God through each other.

Amen

Clarence And Jill
John 15:9-12, 1 Corinthians 12:31-13:13
"Love one another, even as I have loved you."

So few scriptures deal with marriage! Even fewer deal with romantic love. For this reason, we often stretch things, looking for a scripture to fit the occasion. For instance, the only association Jesus had with a wedding is at Cana (John 2). The passage has nothing to do with weddings; it is merely the setting for the first of Jesus' Signs of the Kingdom, so important in Johannine theology. But we read it anyway, and try to say something about weddings and marriage that we can barely sque-e-e-ze from the text.

Similarly, we look for passages dealing with love. The most common text read at weddings, by far, is 1 Corinthians 13. St. Paul was not talking about marriage at all! The occasion for this excursus on the subject of love was an attempt to calm down a feisty congregation that was experiencing in-fighting due to disagreements over the proper place of the various charismatic spiritual gifts. Paul's contention was that no gift was more valuable than Love. But the love he was extolling was the uniquely Godly quality called Agape.

The Text below is another such example. The occasion for Jesus speaking of love (again Agape*), is the beginning of the end of Jesus' time with His disciples. It is part of what has been called the "Farewell Discourse." Be that as it may, when we hear "love," we think "romance." Jesus gives us an opportunity to elevate marriage beyond romance.*

"Love one another, even as I have loved you." That seems an easy enough command to follow for a wedding. And I guess it is easy, if you leave love on a sentimental level. But wait a minute! This is Jesus speaking these words. This is the one who loved us by dying for us because we needed his death — His love, because of sin, our lack of love. How dare we read this passage from the Gospel of John at a wedding? What we are saying is that this relationship, which we consecrate in a Christian wedding, is about Christ's love.

Christ's love is stated something like this: "I love you so much that no matter what you do, I will love you, and accept you as you are, in the hope that you will love me. I am willing to stake my very life on that promise."

Now, how can we promise that: to love no matter what, unto death? Well, we obviously need a greater understanding of love than what our culture gives us normally. Our culture tells us that love is a feeling. Okay, sometimes it is. But mostly, Christian love goes beyond feelings.

Feeling love can be affected by physical and mental health, what and how much you have to eat and drink, what goes on at work, how the kids are behaving, biorhythms, you name it. Feeling love is often largely how you react to your partner's behavior. But Christian love — "Love one another, even as I have loved you." — goes far beyond feelings. Christian love is action.

When St. Paul described Christian love in his first letter to the Corinthians, note if you will, he did not once describe feelings, but actions — ways of being and doing. St. Paul described how to love, and what not to do, if you wish to love. You cannot promise to feel love, but you can promise to do it. You can promise to be faithful, and being faithful is loving.

When Christians marry and promise faithful love, we are saying an amazing thing: "We will love as Christ loved us." That means that we will love not only when our partner is pleasing us, but even when he or she is being a jerk. Christ shows us clearly that it does not take much love when things are pleasant. Love is the necessary, key ingredient when things are unpleasant.

But Christian love does not stop at endurance through tough times. Just as Christ is not only about dying for our sins (though that is the pinnacle of our faith). The miraculous and beautiful truth of God's love for us is that it goes beyond endurance and death for our transgressions, and moves into new life. We gather to celebrate Christian love in marriage, specifically Clarence and Jill's marriage, as something beyond endurance unto death. We celebrate Christ-centered love that moves into new life.

Jill and Clarence pledge that their love will take the joys and the sorrows together, and not only endure them, but make of their life together something beautiful, unexpected, and new. It is this powerful Christian love that we celebrate with them. Together we say that this marriage, and we as a Christian community, not only endure in love, we excel in bringing love to all circumstances.

Given all this, it now seems that Christ's command to love is a tall order ... and it is. You can't do it ... not by your own power, anyhow! Only by the power of the Holy Spirit can we hope to experience the love of Christ, and so receiving that love, give it. Alone, we simply do not have what it takes. But in Christ, and by the power of His Holy Spirit, we can have and give this kind of love. This is our hope and our celebration when we gather as the Christian community today.

Jill and Clarence, it is our hope and prayer that your life together will be a reflection of the love of Christ alive in our world today, and a glimpse of His dominion in the age to come.

Amen

M.J. And Rick
Song of Songs 2:10-13 Psalm 100
Ephesians 5:21-33
John 15:9-12

Now here is a book of the Bible that is about romantic love, and specifically, sex! Some pious folks have been very uncomfortable with this. So uncomfortable are they, that they have tried to say that this is not a love poem, but an allegory of God's love for Israel. Sorry, that is so unlikely it's downright silly! St. Augustine gave us many fine things, but his preoccupation with sex as sin is not one of his gifts for which we ought to be thankful. Yet, we still live with this pietistic legacy. We need to say it loud and clear: sex is not sin!

This poem is included in the Bible as a way of recognizing what a wonderful gift of God human sexuality is. Surely, like all gifts, the greater the gift, the greater the possibility for abusing the gift, and turning it into a curse. But the Church should never call one of God's gifts evil. It is not the gift that is evil, but rather what we do with it.

Since marriage is not only a spiritual, social, and economic union, but a sexual one as well, it is very appropriate to select from this passionate ode one of your scripture readings. As I have already indicated, I use selecting scriptures as part of my pre-marriage counseling routine. Here is a sermon based in part on the Song of Songs.

Also in this sermon is a treatment of Ephesians 5. A commonly read text for weddings, all too commonly it is read without an appropriate comment. That this text has been used to oppress women should not prevent us from reading it, but caution is advised. It does not stand alone well. I believe the preacher is duty-bound to inject here Christ and His liberating Gospel, in order to prevent the abusive, ownership attitude that has been justified by misusing this text.

The most obvious subject for the day has got to be love. But it may surprise you to hear from me that I think it is probably the least understood subject of all that we could talk about.

We know that M.J. and Rick love each other, and we know that they are "in love." But if we left it at that, we would do them and ourselves a great disservice. In the *Song of Songs*, also known as the *Song of Solomon*, we hear of one kind of love. It is the passionate, sexual, moonstruck sort of love that the movies make millions on.

Oooh! That is good stuff! Rejoice and be glad with Rick and M.J. that God has given them that great and awesome gift. Most often we fail to recognize that romance, passion for another, sexual love, is a gift that comes from God. It is! The *Song of Songs* clearly points that out. It is a wonderful and powerful gift.

Because it is powerful, it deserves special treatment and caution. The greater the gift, the greater the responsibility, because it is also true that the greater the gift, the greater the potential for trouble. This kind of love is not enough to base a marriage on. Just having strong feelings for someone is inadequate to the life-long task of marriage.

This passion is subject to all kinds of external and internal forces. It is subject to mood swings, how well things are going at work, physical and mental health, hormonal levels, and just plain time. It is a very vulnerable kind of love. It is based on how you feel, and feelings are not something over which we always have control. So, as good, wonderful and powerful as this great gift of passionate love is, it is not enough.

Yet, I am going to guess that it was this kind of love that you assumed marriage and this wedding were all about. No, that is only part of the story. That is why M.J. and Rick chose more than just this one lesson. There is more love in their relationship than that.

Psalm 100 calls us into this celebration in the presence of God. There is another player here. We declare ourselves to be God's people, sheep of God's pasture. It is also God's love that we celebrate, and God's love endures forever! God's love for us is passionate, but not sexual, and not based on the feelings of the moment. Rather, God's love is based on commitment to a promise. God promises to take care of us, to be with us, no matter what, forever. So too, with us. In marriage, we make these same kinds of promises. We will provide for each other's needs, no matter what, forever.

You might think that would be sufficient. It is a lot, but it is not everything. We need to go further. So, we read on.

Ephesians 5. I get very uncomfortable hearing this text read at weddings. It is often heard as "woman, obey your husband as if he were God." That ain't it! Rick is no god. No man is. This text has too often been used to oppress women instead of free us all to the fullness of God's love. We must hear this text in the reverse order in which it is written to see God's word in it: "Husbands, love your wives, as Christ loved the church and gave himself up for it."

We obey Christ out of His love for us. This has nothing to do with superiority, domination, or the rightful place of women. If Christ is the model of love, then what is described here is mutual respect and love. Surely, that is how Christ loves us. And to understand Christ's love we move to our Gospel lesson.

"Love one another as I have loved you." Those are powerful words! The kind of love that Christ offers is unfailing, unconditional, grace-filled love. It is the kind of love that is based, not on the performance of our beloved, but on our forgiveness. It is not based on how we feel today, but on what we have decided to do. We have decided to promise to love in word and deed, regardless of how we feel.

Even when we are angry, we will love. Even when we have been slighted, we will love. Even when we have been hurt, we will love. Through all that the years will bring, we will love. We may not feel very passionate or sweet, but we will do love anyway.

That does not mean letting your beloved get away with murder. On the contrary. Love includes challenging our beloved when things are not right. Wives, it includes even disobeying your husband, when your husband is wrong. This godly love in a Christian marriage includes loving your spouse enough to be honest with her or him, even though the truth may be painful. It includes trusting your partner with your life.

That is Christian love. That is the love that our savior, Jesus Christ shows us. In spite of fear, in spite of sin, in spite of how we feel about any thing or any one, we promise to forgive and to love, by doing what is best, not only for ourselves, but for our beloved.

The model is, of course, Christ. " . . . as I have loved you" includes the challenges, includes the cross. And of course, it includes the resurrection after the cross that says new life is possible, even after sin and death, because of the love of God in Christ. That is the Christian love that M.J. and Rick, and all Christian marriages, promise.

That is why we are here, celebrating a Christian marriage in a Christian church. We celebrate the gifts of love given to us by God. We celebrate passion, romance, faithfulness, respect, freedom, and above all, we celebrate the love of Christ.

Amen

Denise And Jim
John 15:9-12
Genesis 1:26-31
Ephesians 5:21-33

After a while, every sermon based in the Gospel starts to look the same. This is especially true with weddings. The theme of Christian love versus the love that is espoused by our culture becomes central. Everything else is finding new illustrations and particulars to the couple and families that you are addressing.

As far as we know, Jesus was never married to anyone. But even if he was married, Jesus was not married to the disciples. Yet we read this lesson at weddings: Jesus addressing his disciples, "Love one another even as I have loved you." If Jesus was not talking about marriage, why pick a lesson like this one to be read at a wedding?

Well, frankly, part of the reason is not a very good one. We hear the word "love" and think, for sentimental reasons, this would be a good one to sorta getcha ... right here. We hear the word "love" and we think of romance. But I have never read or heard of an account of Jesus romancing anyone.

There is a really good reason to read this passage at a wedding. It has nothing to do with romance! Now, don't get me wrong, there's nothing wrong with romance! Personally, I would not want to go through life without it. And I am happy for married couples, and even unmarried couples (usually) when they experience romance. But a marriage based solely on romance is doomed to fail.

When romance fails, love takes over. That is what Jesus is talking about when he says, "Love one another, even as I have loved you." Remember how Jesus loves us. It is not with mere sentiment; it is not with romance. Jesus loves us in dying on the cross for us, because we have failed to love him and each other.

Jesus loves us with the love of God that says, "No matter how I feel about how you behave, I will still love you. I will

106

not destroy you, but will give myself to you." That is not some sort of sick, co-dependent kind of thing that needs to be hurt in order to express love, but rather an I-will-never-give-up-on-our-relationship kind of thing. No matter how often we stray, God keeps coming back saying, "I forgive you. I accept you, as you are. Come! Be with me, and together, we will be different — even better — than we are apart!"

There are, to be sure, times when we move away from our relationship with God. We call that sin. When we sin, we damage our relationship with God. If that was all there was to it, we'd be in sorry shape. But God, in our baptism, has said that the covenant made with us in the name of the Father and of the Son and of the Holy Spirit, is an everlasting covenant.

And that is what Christian love, and Christian marriage is all about. That is why we read this passage at weddings. Jim and Denise make promises that go beyond romance, beyond how they feel at any given moment. They promise faithfulness; they give rings as signs of their love and faithfulness; and they do that here, in church, wrapped in the Christian community, reading aloud Christ's commandment to love even as he has loved us. All this, because theirs is also an everlasting covenant.

Theirs is also a covenant not based in the behavior of their partner, but based in loving, forgiving grace. They make promises to love that go far beyond the good times that are ahead. Jim knows this about himself, and knows this about Denise; Denise knows this about herself, and knows this about Jim: they are not marrying perfection. They will need Christ's love. We rejoice with them that they have received this great love, and ask of them, and of God, a great gift: share that love with us.

Jim and Denise, love one another, even as Christ has loved us, not only that your joy may be full and complete, but for our benefit, too. We need your relationship to be a reflection of Christ in our midst, so that in you, we too can experience

Christ's love, and share that love with each other. So it is that we gladly gather with hope and joy, rejoicing in the gift God has given you, praying for you, and pledging our support.

Amen

Steve And Edie
Ephesians 5:21-33

Here is another treatment of Ephesians 5, even more direct.

Anybody here besides me at all troubled by these words from Ephesians? "Wives, be subject to your husbands as you are to the Lord. For the husband is the head of the wife, just as Christ is head of the Church, the body of which He is the savior." There is a lot there to be troubled by, I think!

First of all, the inequality of it. Perhaps I am just too modern in this respect, but I simply do not believe that men are superior to women. And secondly, how could you possibly compare the role of the husband to the role of Christ? Never have I seen a husband who came anywhere close to filling the role of Savior! Edie knows Steve well enough to not expect perfection, much less salvation from him. And there is no apology necessary; it is a totally unrealistic expectation for any human, male or female, to save another, as Christ has saved us. So what is this passage about, and how does it apply to Steve and Edie's wedding?

We are so taken aback by these words that we miss the mutuality that is being expressed here. The very first line, we miss! "Be subject to one another out of reverence for Christ." A successful marriage needs that. It is a partnership in which the husband and the wife are subject to each other. Neither the man nor the woman simply goes off capriciously doing his or her thing, and leaving the spouse in the dust. Rather, there is communication, give and take, compromise, and above all, love.

When I say love, I mean Christian love, and this is quite different from much of what we see in the world. Read on in this lesson from Ephesians, and you will see what I mean. "Husbands, love your wives, just as Christ loved the Church, and gave himself up for her." You see, wives can be subject to their husbands, if their husbands will love their wives with the love of Christ.

It is not hard to be subject to one another if the other, husband or wife, is willing to die for his or her partner. And that is what Christian marriage and Christian love is about. It is about saying to your partner, with everything you've got, "I give my life to you."

It is three things: It is sacrificial, it is grace-filled, it is unconditional.

Sacrificial: "I will give up many things in order to make our relationship work. Anything that interferes with our being united in Christ, I will give up. Anything that weakens our relationship, I will sacrifice. And anything that is good for us, I will take on." This is Christian love, because that is exactly what Jesus Christ does for us. Christ gave up his life for us. Christ took our sins and disposed of them.

Christian love and marriage are grace-filled, that is, it is merciful. The Lord does not hold the sacrifice of Christ on the cross against us. He does not say, "See what I did for you? Now, pay up!" No, God is content to merely sweep us off our feet with love. The sacrifice is made in love and is offered to us free of charge, simply out of love.

Marriage needs this most of all. Marriage needs forgiveness, grace. None of us will be the perfect partner. No one, husband or wife, will be so Christ-like as to be found without fault. Everyone has bad days. The cure for sin is forgiveness ... we learn that from God, through Christ.

This kind of Christian love is unconditional. Acceptance, forgiveness, and sacrifice are unconditional acts of love. They are given purely out of love, no strings attached, and no price tag. It is a gift, pure and simple. This is not the way people usually behave. It is not easy. But it is the Christ-model of love.

The purpose of this sacrificial, gracious, unconditional love? New Life. The death of Christ is not the end of the story. The story goes on to the Resurrection. Jesus Christ died and was raised from the dead that we might have new life. And this too, is what Christian love is about, and how the writer of Ephesians can dare to make the comparison between marriage and the Church's relationship with Christ.

We marry in order to pledge something new, something quite different than we were before. In marriage, we are committed to living in Christ, loving in a way that is only possible by the power of the Holy Spirit. In marriage, we pledge to live a new life of love that is sacrificial, gracious, and unconditional. We pledge to die to ourselves, and rise to new life together, as long as life endures.

Amen

Marty And Jane
John 15:9-12, 1 Corinthians 13:1-7,13

No matter how you slice it, marriage will always change people. Psychologists say that change always involves grief. Therefore, grief is always a part of marriage. Sometimes, as with a close-knit family, this is the central dynamic in a new marriage: "What will happen to our relationship now?" Family dynamics may be an important subject to address from the pulpit.

Love changes everything. When a man and woman decide to love one another in marriage, many things change. Life is not solitary or independent, but a new partnership. You gain some things and you lose some things. You get the goodness of the combined strength that comes in a partnership. You lose independence. In faithfulness and togetherness, you get security, and support, and you lose some of that togetherness that you had with others. Many, if not all, of your relationships change.

The decision to love someone, anyone, is a decision to change, and with that comes a necessary loss. Our Lord, Jesus, says, "Love one another, even as I have loved you." Restated, that could be read as, "Change one another, and submit yourself to change." Why bother? Because it is worth the pain!

Christ loves us in the loss of his life. That certainly was no easy change for him. But he obviously thought it was worth it. We obviously receive and benefit a great deal from Christ's loss of life. But we are also changed. We cannot receive and return Christ's love without incurring necessary losses.

Christian marriage is about Christ-like love. "Love one another as I have loved you." In other words, "Die to yourself for one another."

But love is not only the cause of grief, it is also the solution. Love fills to overflowing the cup that empties itself. That is also Christ. Through the loss of His life came also the gain of New Life. Eternal life.

A different kind of new life today is given to Marty and Jane. We join in giving them that new life. They give love to each other. We give love to them. Together, we receive Christ's love in Holy Communion.

All of it is with some sense of loss. And all of it is with an even greater sense of gain.

Amen

Kathleen And Lodi
Genesis 2:18-24
Matthew 19:4-6

Genesis 2 is a common wedding text, and unlike some we might read, actually is about marriage. Though an ancient writing, it still holds great meaning for the believer, even if the believer is not inclined toward a literal understanding of the scriptures. The wonderful young couple that chose this text epitomized a mature loving relationship. It was a joy to have had the privilege of ministering to them.

What a great and clever God we have! Intentionally making us wanting, incomplete, so that we would need each other. God could have made us whole, complete, perfect from the start, but what good would that do? Imagine yourself to be 100 percent self-sufficient, if you will. You would not love, nor desire to be loved. You would be alone, and what is worse, you would not care. You would be a totally self-centered and narrow-minded creature.

Instead, God made us in the image of the divine: One who is not content to be alone; One who seeks to share life with others; One who wants to love and to be loved. God made us needful. That idea is expressed wonderfully in our lesson from Genesis.

God took the one creature, and made another — like the first, but different. God made us to be lacking just what our partner has to offer. God made us incomplete, so we would desire the partnership of another, knowing that it was "not good for [us] to be alone."

This is not to say that being single is somehow wrong, or inferior. Not at all. God has love for us all, and for some, being single is as appropriate, or even more appropriate, than marriage. But for Kathleen and Lodi, it is not so.

Symbolized in the rib, the man was made to be incomplete without the woman, so that completeness might not be found in isolation, but in relationship to others.

Did I say completeness? Not by a long shot! No, God was smarter than that still. In infinite wisdom, God made us not only needful of each other, but needful of God, as well. The Lord made us such that completeness, wholeness, would not be found in any relationship unless it was in relationship with God, as well. We were made lacking so that we would desire God's presence in everything. We were made such that if we enter into a relationship with another, as good as it may be, we would still need God's presence to make it work, to make it complete, and truly fulfilling. God loves us that much.

Our Creator loves us enough to make us incomplete, that we might seek wholeness. God loves us enough to go to great lengths to get intimate with us. It is a famous verse: "God so loved the world, that He gave us His only begotten Son . . . ." (John 3:16). And that is finally what we need most of all: the love of God through Jesus Christ.

That is why we have weddings in church. We call everyone's attention to the fact that Lodi and Kathleen, who are married today, are needful of one thing: God's love. And this is why you are all here: as the People of God, you come to help them. You come to offer your support, and encouragement, and to lift them in the presence of God, that they may there find fulfillment.

Here in the Church, they will be united in Christ. That is a great word, "united." It means to make a unit; to make two separate things into one. That is the theme in the lessons Kathleen and Lodi chose for their wedding: two become one. And in Christ, they are made one. God chooses to unite them that they might enjoy a fulfilled life in Christ.

Amen

Cathi And Jim
1 Corinthians 13:1-13

Whenever presiding at a wedding, I need to remind myself that there are doubtless a lot of non-believers in the congregation that day. There will probably be many who attend worship only on the occasion of weddings and funerals, and perhaps Christmas and Easter. They may come expecting to enjoy a nice cultural expression of what marriage may be about, and they will doubtless be there carrying their own baggage from their personal experiences with marriage, either as a spouse, or as a child. Again, it is then, especially, that I must remember that my job as a minister is to preside at worship, and to preach the Gospel.

When they brand cattle, they leave a mark on the animal's rump that says: "This cow belongs to me!" That is how many people view the exchange of wedding rings: "Here! Wear this ring. That'll tell everybody that you are mine." That is exactly backwards from the way things should be, and exactly the opposite, I am happy to tell you, from the way things are in this marriage.

The rings do not mean, "You belong to me," nor do they mean, "No trespassing. Keep out!" Rather, the ring is given as a sign of love and faithfulness on the part of the one who gives the ring. With the ring goes not a claim on a piece of property, but a pledge, a promise, a covenant. Jim and Cathi are making promises to each other today. They are establishing a covenant. The rings are physical reminders of the promises made to each other: life-long love and faithfulness.

Now, what does it mean to pledge love? How can you pledge a feeling? What is more, how can you pledge a loving, warm, romantic feeling when you know that there will be, in any and every marriage, times of anger, sadness, and conflict? How can you pledge to forever feel love? Answer: You cannot.

So what is going on? 1 Corinthians 13 is going on. The whole reading is love, love, love, but never once has St. Paul mentioned a feeling. Paul speaks of the love of Christ — God's love. God's love is not a feeling. It is a choice to act in spite of feelings. It is the kind of love that is possible even with enemies! And if this love is possible with enemies, surely it is possible between such good friends as Cathi and Jim.

God's greatest expression of love is in Jesus Christ. In Christ, God forgives us. When your partner hurts you, you forgive. That is a promise of love that you can keep. It does not mean that you won't feel hurt. Christ was certainly hurt — even killed, but still, it was in this death that God loves us and forgives us. Promising this kind of forgiving love does not mean that you will ignore what your partner did to hurt you, nor that you will not feel angry. It means that in spite of how you feel, you will choose to love and forgive.

That is the kind of love God has promised you. It is the promise made in the covenant of Christ on the cross. And that is what this marriage is all about — a covenant of love.

Why enter into such a covenant? Aren't we better off not making such promises? Aren't we better off being less vulnerable than that? If Christ is the model of love, look what it got Him! He was betrayed by one of His best friends, and tortured to death! Who needs love if it means such pain?

We do. The covenant of Christ not only took Jesus to the cross and grave, it took Him to the Resurrection: to New Life. You cannot have Easter without Good Friday. The New Covenant is both the death and the Resurrection. This new covenant of Jim and Cathi's is very much like the New Covenant in Christ.

There will be suffering. There will be loss. In the end, there will even be physical death. But in the love — Godly love — that they pledge to one another today, there is so much more. There is new life.

Through forgiveness, love will raise them from pain and suffering and even death, and bring them to new life together. We celebrate this great joy with them today. We rejoice in the new covenant of Cathi and Jim.

Amen

Karl And Wendi
John 15:9-12

The nature of communal worship and communal support is expressed best in the sacrament of Holy Communion. Whenever practical and desired by the couple, I encourage the celebration of the Eucharist surrounding this business of the Church marriage. Here is a sermon where this was especially the case.

In this particular situation, there were some important family dynamics at work, as well. There were feelings of non-acceptance for both sets of in-laws, and some religious conflicts. In this case, the ministry of worship leadership, reconciliation, and preaching were, as always, not just for the bride and groom, but the entire congregation.

In the name of the Father, and of the Son, and of the Holy Spirit. Amen.

I've always wanted to begin a wedding ceremony in the way of the old tradition. You know, like in the movies. "Dearly Beloved, we are gathered here in the presence of Almighty God, to unite Wendi and Karl in the state of Holy Matrimony." It seems just too hokey! But it is exactly right, too. It is precisely why we are here.

This is a special occasion. Wendi and Karl wanted all of their family and friends to come and be a part of this. You were invited not just to watch, but to participate; to sing songs, and hear scripture lessons about faithfulness, love, hope and joy. They wanted the people who are important to them to share in today's sacred occasion.

Karl and Wendi also wanted all of their important people to share in their unity. Today they are united in Christ in two special ways. First, they will be united by commitment. They will exchange vows, or promises, to be true to one another in all circumstances, until death parts them.

Secondly, they will unite in Christ in Holy Communion. Together, they will experience a spiritual unity in the Body and

Blood of our Lord and Savior, Jesus Christ. This is made all the more special, because today is Karl's first Holy Communion.

If you normally receive Holy Communion in your Christian Church, you are also invited to receive the sacrament. In this, you join with Wendi and Karl in the One who makes us one: Jesus Christ. It is a powerful thing.

Karl and Wendi are made one, and we are made one, in Christ. The unity we share with each other is a permanent bond. It is as serious a commitment as we can make. Together, we are saying that this is not just Wendi and Karl's "thing." This is our responsibility, together. All of us: "Dearly Beloved, we are gathered here today, in the presence of Almighty God, to unite ... " The whole Church, all families and friends, and above all, Christ, we are all committed to actively supporting and sustaining the unity this couple shares, and we share, today.

Central to this relationship in Christ is forgiveness. In Holy Communion, by the Body and Blood of Christ, we receive forgiveness of sins. We, in turn, forgive one another. We accept Karl and Wendi as one with us. In-laws accept new family members as their own. And though you may at times disagree and even not like one another, you will, in Christ, forgive, accept, and love one another.

That is today's Gospel lesson. Jesus gives us the command to love one another as He loved us. That is not limited to Wendi and Karl, nor is it limited to when you feel good about your mate. To love in Christ means all the time, even when you would rather not be around the other — love, as Christ loved us. That is rooted in forgiveness.

This is the love of God: forgiveness. It is how we are made one with God: in forgiveness through Jesus Christ on the cross. It is also how we become and remain one in our relationships — through love that is expressed most deeply and completely in forgiveness.

Karl, Wendi, make that Godly love in Christ central to your relationship, and we will rejoice with you in your discovery of abundant life in Christ.

Amen

Dean And Judy
Psalm 100

Don't overlook the Psalms as a source for readings and songs fit for a wedding. But, as always, caution is advised. Psalms 127 and 128 are wonderful (though perhaps a trifle sexist) for a wedding, but totally inappropriate for a couple that does not intend, or will not be able, to have children. The sermon which follows was for one such couple. Entering into their second marriage, and no longer "young," other subjects were more important.

Dean and Judy, you wanted to be married in the Church. What does that mean? It is more than just a nice romantic location. We are all doing something very important here. When we marry in the Church, we put marriage in the Christian context. That means that for you, being married will be a reflection of Christ, a reflection of God.

The Psalm we just read concludes:

"For the Lord is good; his mercy is everlasting, and his faithfulness endures from age to age." (RSV)

That is the vision! In your marriage, we will see God! As God is good to His creation, you will be good to each other. As God's mercy is everlasting, you will be merciful to each other, forgiving each other, time and time again. As God's faithfulness endures from age to age, so you will be faithful to each other.

And you people who came here to church to participate in this wedding, there is great meaning for you, as well! You are not just spectators! You pledge support and faithfulness as family and friends; as the People of God. You just recited: "We are His people, and the sheep of His pasture." That makes God's business our business.

Today we will eat the bread and share the cup: the Body and Blood of Christ. In sharing this meal, we share in the life, death, and rising of Christ. It is death to the old way of life, and rising to new life. It is in this context that Judy and Dean are today wed. And that means everything.

Listen carefully as we worship together. The prayers, the vows, the exchange of the peace, the hymns, the sacrament, the benediction — it all applies to us, and to this marriage.

Dean and Judy are not entering into this marriage lightly, but with much preparation. They have not only prepared for this wedding, but more importantly, they have prepared for their marriage. They have come to know each other very well. They have shared on a level that reaches toward their greatest depths and their inmost being; they have shared each other's souls.

Judy and Dean, it is my hope and prayer, and my charge to you: continue to fearlessly face each other, confront your issues, and above all, communicate as openly and as deeply as you are able. You have read and studied and worked together to gain an understanding of what your marriage in the Church means. Today, you enter joyfully into the life-long sharing of one another's lives, all aspects, both positive and negative. The joy you will experience will be proportionate to your keeping alive the vision of the Godly life together.

In trying to write your own vows, you both came to the conclusion that all you could come up with seemed to be an imitation of the old traditional vows. Judy said, "I mean, 'till death do us part,' how could you say it any better than that?" So it is that they have chosen these vows. They are powerful promises.

The one that encompasses them all is this: "Will you love each other?" Maybe it is as the song goes, "I don't know how to love him (or her)." That is the task before you: find out!

"Will you love each other?" You know, it is a promise that in one sense you cannot keep. You cannot promise how you will feel. Emotions don't work that way. You cannot truthfully say that no matter what is done or said, or whatever else may happen, "I will love you." You don't know!

But you can promise to love. Love in this sense is a verb — an action verb. And that you can promise. To love each other even as Christ loves us — to death — is a promise we can make and, by the power of God, keep. To forbear, to support, to provide, to care for, to be faithful, to endure, and above all, to forgive when promises are broken, this you can promise. And this is what a Church wedding means.

Amen

Recommended Readings

Campolo, Tony. *Wake Up America! Answering God's Radical Call While Living in the Real World.* Harper San Francisco: San Francisco, CA, 1991.

Celebrating Marriage: Preparing the Wedding Liturgy: a workbook for engaged couples. Paul Covino, editor, Lawrence Madden, Elaine Rendler, John Buscemi. Washington, D.C.: Pastoral Press, c1987.

A Christian Celebration of Marriage. The Consultation on Common Texts. Philadelphia: Fortress Press, 1987.

Countryman, L. William. *Dirt, Greed, and Sex: Sexual ethics in the New Testament, and their implications for today.* Philadelphia: Fortress Press, 1988.

Dell, Edward Thomas. *A Handbook for Church Weddings.* New York: Morehouse-Barlow Co, 1964. (An Episcopalian guide to marriage ministry and practice.)

Friedman, Edwin H., *Generation to Generation: Family Process In Church and Synagogue.* New York: The Guilford Press, 1985.

Kelleher, Stephen Joseph. *Divorce and Remarriage for Catholics?* Garden City, New York: Image Books, 1976.

Kirschenbaum, Howard. *The Wedding Book: alternative ways to celebrate marriage.* by Howard Kirschenbaum and Rockwell Stensrud. New York: Seabury Press, 1974.

Likness, Lawrence R. *With Your Promises: Planning Your Marriage Service.* Minneapolis: Augsburg Publishing House, 1980.

Mueller, Charles S. *Planning a Christian Wedding Service: a planning resource for the parents.* St. Louis: Concordia Publishing House, 1981.

Panati, Charles. *Extraordinary Endings of Practically Everything and Everybody*. New York: HarperCollins, 1989.

Pfatteicher, Philip H. and Messerli, Carlos R. *Manual on the Liturgy: Lutheran Book of Worship*. Minneapolis: Augsburg Publishing House, 1979.

Ramshaw, Elaine. *Ritual and Pastoral Care*. Don S. Browning, ed., Philadelphia: Fortress Press, 1987.

Schillebeeckx, Edward. *Marriage: Human Reality and Saving Mystery*. Translated by N.D. Smith. New York: Sheed and Ward, 1965.

Bibliography

Adams, Clifford Rose. *Preparing for Marriage; a guide to marital and sexual adjustment.* New York: Dutton, 1951.

Bainton, Roland Herbert. *What Christianity Says About Sex, Love and Marriage.* New York: Association Press, 1957.

The Book of Common Prayer. 1976 edition. New York: The Seabury Press.

Borning Cry: Worship for a New Generation. Compiled by John Carl Ylvisaker. Published by Ylvisaker. Distributed by ColorSongTM Productions, Inc. Box 120321, St. Paul, MN 55112, c1991.

Bowman, Henry Adelbert. *Marriage for Moderns.* 7th ed. New York: McGraw-Hill, 1974.

Briffault, Robert, and Bronislaw Malinowski. *Marriage, Past and Present.* Boston: Porter Sargent Publisher, 1956.

Bryant, Flora F. *It's Your Wedding; a complete wedding guide for making the most important day of your life the most beautiful and memorable day.* by Flora F.T., and Kendall S. Bryant. New York: Cowles Book Co, 1970.

Campolo, Tony. *Wake Up America! Answering God's Radical Call While Living in the Real World.* Harper San Francisco: San Francisco, CA, 1991.

Celebrating Marriage: Preparing the Wedding Liturgy: a workbook for engaged couples. Paul Covino, editor, Lawrence Madden, Elaine Rendler, John Buscemi. Washington, D.C.: Pastoral Press, c1987.

A Christian Celebration of Marriage. The Consultation on Common Texts. Philadelphia: Fortress Press, 1987.

The Cokesbury Marriage Manual. Ed. by William H. Leach. 2nd. Rev. Ed. New York, Nashville: Abingdon-Cokesbury Press, 1945.

Countryman, L. William. *Dirt, Greed, and Sex: Sexual ethics in the New Testament, and their implications for today.* Philadelphia: Fortress Press, 1988.

Dell, Edward Thomas. *A Handbook for Church Weddings.* New York: Morehouse-Barlow Co, 1964. (An Episcopalian guide to marriage ministry and practice.)

Determining Needs in Your Youth Ministry. Search Institute. Published by Group Books, Inc. Several studies available on national to local levels. Search Institute. 122 W. Franklin Avenue. Minneapolis, MN. 55404.

Eickhoff, Andrew R. *A Christian View of Sex and Marriage.* New York: Free Press, 1966.

Fielding, William John. *Strange Customs of Courtship and Marriage.* Philadelphia: Blakiston, 1942.

Five Hymn Improvisations for Wedding and General Use. Arranged by Paul Manz. St. Louis: Morning Star Publishers, 1989. Publisher's no.: MSM-10-850.

Friedman, Edwin H. *Generation to Generation: Family Process In Church and Synagogue.* New York: The Guilford Press, 1985.

Frysell, Regina Homen. *Wedding Music.* American Guild of Organists. Rock Island, IL: Augustana Press, 1956.

Hauerwas, Stanley. *A Community of Character: Toward A Constructive Christian Social Ethic.* Notre Dame, Indiana: University of Notre Dame Press, 1981.

The Hymnal. Church Hymnal Corporation. 800 Second Avenue, New York, NY 10017. 1982.

Jenson, Robert. "The Sacraments." from Braaten, Carl E., ed., and Jenson, Robert ed., *Christian Dogmatics.* Vol. II Locusio, part two. Philadelphia: Fortress Press, 1984.

Johnson, Wendell Stacy. *Sex and Marriage in Victorian Poetry.* Ithaca, NY: Cornell University Press, 1975.

Kelleher, Stephen Joseph. *Divorce and Remarriage For Catholics?* Garden City, New York: Image Books, 1976.

Kirschenbaum, Howard. *The Wedding Book: alternative ways to celebrate marriage.* by Howard Kirschenbaum and Rockwell Stenstud. New York: Seabury Press, 1974.

Lazarus. *Wedding Embassy Yearbook.* Columbus, OH: Embassy Pub. Co., 1964.

Likness, Lawrence R. *With Your Promises: Planning Your Marriage Service.* Minneapolis, MN: Augsburg Publishing House, 1980.

Luther, Martin, 1483-1546. *Luther's Marriage Ring. A selection of three sermons of Martin Luther on the marriage estate.* Translated by J. Sheatsley. Columbus, OH: Lutheran Book Concern, 1904.

The Lutheran Book of Worship. Philadelphia: Augsburg Publishing House, and Board of Publication, Lutheran Church in America, Philadelphia. c1978.

Mace, David Robert. *Getting Ready for Marriage.* Nashville: Abingdon Press, 1972.

Maier, Walter Arthur. *For Better, Not for Worse: a manual of Christian Matrimony.* St. Louis, MO: Concordia Publishing House, 1935.

National Research Council. *Risking the Future: Adolescent Sexuality, Pregnancy, and Childbearing.* Cheryl D. Hayes, Editor. Washington, D.C.: National Academy Press, 1987.

Panati, Charles. *Extraordinary Origins of Everyday Things.* New York: HarperCollins, 1987.

Panait, Charles. *Extraordinary Endings of Practically Everything and Everybody.* New York: HarperCollins, 1989.

Plutarch. "Romulus." *Plutarch's Lives.* Edited by Raymond T. Bond. Tudor Publishing Company, 1935.

Ramshaw, Elaine. *Ritual and Pastoral Care*. Don S. Browning, ed., Philadelphia: Fortress Press, 1987

Schillebeeckx, Edward. *Marriage: Human Reality and Saving Mystery*. Translated by N.D. Smith. New York: Sheed and Ward, 1965.

Seidenberg, Robert. *Marriage in Life and Literature*. New York: Philosophical Library, 1970.

Stevenson, Kenneth. *Nuptial Blessing: A Study of Christian Marriage Rites*. New York: Oxford University Press, 1983.

Swadley, Elizabeth. *Your Christian Wedding*. Nashville, TN: Broadman Press, 1966.

Tannahill, Reay. *Sex In History*. New York: Stein and Day Publishers, 1980.

Thielicke, Helmut. *The Ethics of Sex*. Translated by John W. Doberstein. New York: Harper and Row, 1964.

Endnotes

Preface

1. Fielding, William John. *Strange Customs of Courtship and Marriage*. Philadelphia: Blakiston, 1942.

2. Stevenson, Kenneth. *Nuptial Blessing: A Study of Christian Marriage Rites*. New York. Oxford University Press. 1983, and Thielicke, Helmut. *The Ethics of Sex*. Translated by John W. Doberstein. New York: Harper and Row, 1964.

3. Fielding, William John. Previously cited.

4. Bainton, Roland Herbert. *What Christianity Says About Sex, Love and Marriage*. New York: Association Press, 1957.

Chapter One
"Customary, But Stupid!"

1. Fielding, William John. *Strange Customs of Courtship and Marriage*. Philadelphia: Blakiston, 1942.

2. Briffault, Robert, and Bronislaw Malinowski. *Marriage, Past and Present*. Boston: Porter Sargent Publisher, 1956.

3. Tannahill, Reay. *Sex In History*. New York: Stein and Day Publishers, 1980.

4. Panati, Charles. *Extraordinary Endings of Practically Everything and Everybody*. New York: HarperCollins, 1989.

5. *Prepare/Enrich Newsletter*. Dr. Kenneth Stewart and Dr. David Olson. Minneapolis, MN: Prepare-Enrich, Inc., Vol. 2, No. 2. Fall 1988.

6. National Research Council. *Risking the Future: Adolescent Sexuality, Pregnancy, and Childbearing*. Cheryl D. Hayes, Editor. Washington, D.C.: National Academy Press, 1987.

7. Hauerwas, Stanley. *A Community of Character: Toward a Constructive Christian Social Ethic.* 1981. University of Notre Dame Press. Notre Dame, IN. See especially part III: "The Church and Social Policy: The Family, Sex, and Abortion."

8. Countryman, L. William. *Dirt, Greed, and Sex: Sexual ethics in the New Testament, and their implications for today.* Philadelphia: Fortress Press, 1988.

9. Panati, Charles. Previously cited.

10. Fielding, William John. Previously cited.

11. Briffault, Robert, and Bronislaw Malinowski. Previously cited.

12. Fielding, William John. Previously cited.

13. *The Cokesbury Marriage Manual.* Ed. by William H. Leach. 2nd. Rev. Ed. New York, Nashville: Abingdon-Cokesbury Press, 1945.

14. *The Book of Common Prayer.* 1976 edition. New York: The Seabury Press.

15. Maier, Walter Arthur. *For Better, Not for Worse: a manual of Christian matrimony.* St. Louis, MO: Concordia Publishing House, 1935.

16. Panati, Charles. *Extraordinary Origins of Everyday Things.* New York: HarperCollins, 1987.

17. Panati, Charles. Cited above, and Fielding, William John. Previously cited.

18. Kirschenbaum, Howard. *The Wedding Book: alternative ways to celebrate marriage.* by Howard Kirschenbaum and Rockwell Stensrud. New York: Seabury Press, 1974.

19. Panati, Charles. *Extraordinary Origins of Everyday Things.* Previously cited.

20. Panati, Charles. Cited above.

21. *Celebrating Marriage: Preparing the Wedding Liturgy: a workbook for engaged couples.* Paul Covino, editor, Lawrence Madden, Elaine Rendler, John Buscemi. Washington D.C.: Pastoral Press, c1987.

22. Plutarch. "Romulus." *Plutarch's Lives.* Edited by Raymond T. Bond. Tudor Publishing Company, 1935.

Chapter Two
"Making It A Sacred Occassion"

1. *The Lutheran Book of Worship.* 1978. Philadelphia: Augsburg Publishing House, and Board of Publication, Lutheran Church in America, c1978.

2. Arnold, Matthew. "Dover Beach," from Johnson, Wendell Stacy. *Sex and Marriage in Victorian Poetry.* Ithaca, NY: Cornell University Press, 1975.

3. *Borning Cry: Worship for a New Generation.* Compiled by John Carl Ylvisaker. Published by Ylvisaker. Distributed by ColorSongTM Productions, Inc. Box 120321, St. Paul, MN. 55112, c1991.

4. *The Hymnal.* Church Hymnal Corporation. 800 Second Avenue, New York, NY. 10017, 1982.

5. Swadley, Elizabeth. *Your Christian Wedding.* Nashville: Broadman Press, 1966.

6. Jenson, Robert. from Braaten, Carl E., ed. and Jenson, Robert W., ed., *Christian Dogmatics.* Vol. II, Locus 10, Part Two: "The Sacraments." Philadelphia: Fortress Press, 1984. see also pp. 383-5.

7. Schillebeeckx, Edward. *Marriage: Human Reality and Saving Mystery.* Translated by N.D. Smith. New York: Sheed and Ward, 1965.

8. Schillebeeckx, Edward. Cited above.

Chapter Three
"Premarital Counseling: Insist On It!"

1. Arnold, Matthew. "Dover Beach," from Johnson, Wendell Stacy. *Sex and Marriage in Victorian Poetry.* Ithaca, NY: Cornell University Press, 1975.

2. Mace, David Robert. *Getting Ready for Marriage.* Nashville: Abingdon Press, 1972.

3. Mace, David Robert. Cited above.

4. Bowman, Henry Adelbert. *Marriage for Moderns.* 7th ed. New York: McGraw-Hill, 1974.

5. Adams, Clifford Rose. *Preparing for Marriage; a guide to marital and sexual adjustment.* New York: Dutton, 1951.

6. Arnold, Matthew. "Switzerland" from Johnson, Wendell Stacy. *Sex and Marriage in Victorian Poetry.* Ithaca, NY: Cornell University Press, 1975.

7. Prepare/Enrich Inc., P.O. Box 190, Minneapolis, MN. 55458-0190.

8. Friedman, Edwin H. *Generation to Generation: Family Process In Church and Synagogue.* New York: The Guilford Press, 1985.

Chapter Four
"Fee? Fee?"

1. and 2. *The Cokesbury Marriage Manual.* Ed. by William H. Leach. 2nd Rev. ed. New York, NY., Nashville: Abingdon-Cokesbury Press, 1945.

3. Schillebeeckx, Edward. *Marriage: Human Reality and Saving Mystery.* Translated by N.D. Smith. New York: Sheed and Ward, 1965. (p. 255).

Chapter Five
"Inexpensive, Not Cheap"

1. Lazarus. *Wedding Embassy Yearbook*. Columbus, OH: Embassy Pub. Co., 1964.

2. Campolo, Tony. *Wake Up America! Answering God's Radical Call While Living in the Real World*. San Francisco: Harper SanFrancisco, 1991.

Chapter Six
"Presents Or Presence?"

1. Fielding, William John. *Strange Customs of Courtship and Marriage*. Philadelphia: Blakiston, 1942.

2. (Oh, all right! If you really want to see one!) Page 77 of: Bryant, Flora F. *It's Your Wedding; a complete wedding guide for making the most important day of your life the most beautiful and memorable day.* by Flora F.T., and Kendall S. Bryant. New York: Cowles Book Co, 1970.

Appendix C
"Sermons You Can Use"

1. Luther, Martin. "Marriage Sermon," based on Hebrews 13:4. *Luther's Marriage Ring. A Selection of Three Sermons of Dr. Martin Luther on the Marriage Estate.* Translated from the German by Rev. J. Sheatsley. Columbus, OH: Lutheran Book Concern, 1904.